Keith Arthur

Fishing

*The best excuse
for loafing
in the countryside...*

GreenUmbrella
Publishing

This edition first published in the UK in 2009
By Green Umbrella Publishing

© Green Umbrella Publishing 2009

www.gupublishing.co.uk

Publishers Jules Gammond and Vanessa Gardner

Creative Director: Kevin Gardner

Printed and bound by J F Print Ltd., Sparkford, Somerset

ISBN: 978-1-906635-35-0

Keith
Arthur

None of what you are about to read would have happened without the help, encouragement and occasionally whip-cracking of the following: David Hall, whose original Coarse Fisherman magazine published my first article and then introduced me to Micky Shepherd who produced and directed my first angling videos that drew Wire TV to invite me to appear on Fisherman's Tales which was then picked up by Sky Sports and converted to Tight Lines with Bruno Brookes who taught me what I know about presenting. That in turn made Barry Hearn decide he wanted to manage me and once that ball was rolling Barry got me the gig on TalkSPORT with Fisherman's Blues. My thanks and eternal gratitude go to all of them as well as everyone who appears either extant or posthumously within the following chapters.

Keith Arthur

Contents

Keith Arthur

Prologue

I have been fishing for as long as I can remember – well, almost, as I can recall being held in my maternal grandmother's arms while the firemen rushed past to put out the chimney fire in the house of my birth, in Axminster Road, Holloway, London N7. As I was told we moved from there when I was two-and-a-half and still an 'only child', (my three sisters came later), I probably hadn't yet been lured by the art of angling.

Fishing had snagged me by at least the age of six, even if it was only with a net. I'm sure it would have been earlier but no one in my immediate family had ever partaken – the closest relative who fished was the father of my afore-mentioned grandmother: 'Grandpa Rocky' – so I was treading new ground.

There is a wonderful family story that revolves around Grandpa Rocky, Rocky being the old family name, and his predilection with angling. He was employed as what would be called 'security' these days, in Plymouth Naval Dockyard. He fished whenever he could and one of my favourite stories was how he caught a conger eel and brought it home in a sack, apparently dead. In reality it was a long way from the Pearly Gates, escaping from the sack which had been secreted in the outside toilet and writhing around the back yard: '… barking like a dog', the story goes.

I know that congers do make a sort of grunting sound *in extremis,* which may or may not sound like a barking dog, so the tale may well be true.

Fishing

Keith Arthur

However, the main story revolving around Grandpa Rocky was that, whilst fishing, he lost a submarine that he should have been guarding. I've not been able to find evidence that confirms or denies the tale but, as legend has it, whilst he was attending to his conger tackle rather than keeping guard, a submarine disappeared. Obviously this would be a rather touchy subject for His Majesty's Navy in those days, which is probably why I can find no record of the event, but the way the story runs in our family is that German divers nicked it and sunk it in the depths of Plymouth Sound.

I have to confess that I have not been involved in anything as dramatic as losing a Naval warship but I have skipped responsibilities in the past to go fishing: responsibilities such as school, work, honeymoon and wedding anniversaries and those tales, all true, are related herein.

This book is not an autobiography but it is autobiographical: it's not my life but things that have happened during it in and around times when I was fishing, if that makes any sense.

I have mentioned quite a few people, all of them friends, some of them no longer with us. I hope my words raise happy memories for those that knew them. Most of the fellow-anglers mentioned are alive and I hope that I haven't crucially embarrassed them – slightly is fine, badly was not my intention. It is my wish that some of the stories remind them of what great times we had when we were younger.

Keith Arthur

Finsbury Park

There wasn't much in the way of countryside in Holloway but a mile away, up the Seven Sisters Road, was Finsbury Park. To a small child it was enormous and had loads of grass, football pitches, including a couple of 'red cinder' specials that skinned more knees than the eel skinner at Manze's Pie Shop did eels, and a boating lake. It was the lake that caught my imagination as, when I walked around it, I saw people fishing.

It certainly wasn't easy to fish as the rules stated that crossing the waist-high iron railings that surrounded the entire lake was NOT allowed so the people fishing had to fish over them.

When my first fishing rod and reel arrived, courtesy of a birthday present, I couldn't wait to get to the park and fish. I remember the rod well: it was manufactured using 'smoked cane'; bamboo that had what looked like cigarette burns along it, with twisted wire guides bound on with red thread, and a thicker, wooden handle fitted with two metal collars to hold the reel.

The reel itself was bakelite with a single, green handle with some kind of braided line spooled on it. I also had a float; a tapered object with a couple of inches of red paint at one end, a small, metal tray of split lead shot and a packet of five hooks, large enough for cod, never mind what might be swimming around Finsbury Park Lake. I suspect that this was the equivalent of today's 'starter outfits' that also contain tackle not quite fit for the purpose intended but sufficiently good to stir the interest of aspiring anglers.

Bait was required and, as a boy, that means bread or worms. Bread, until enough knowledge is gained to use it correctly, is a most unreliable ally. It is on the hook when cast out but never when reeling in. The great thing as a child is assuming that the bread has gone because a fish has eaten it. Both of those, taken individually, are possibly correct: the bread has gone and a fish has eaten it. It's the 'because' that is doubtful.

Worms, on the other hand, stay on once hooked. However, a hooked worm stays when the tackle is retrieved, so the assumption is that nothing wants to eat it. Bread, therefore, becomes the bait of choice until a fish is caught on worms.

The most successful angler at the lake was 'Old Joe'. He had a rod far longer than any of the boys and a nose far longer and more hooked than any I have seen since. It is highly likely that the original Mr Punch was a caricature of Old Joe. He also wore a red beret and was always fishing the same spot; opposite the end of the island to the right of the boathouse, from where rowing boats could be hired. There was, of course, no fishing from the boats, or from the landing stage used to launch them.

Joe's tackle, his float and hooks, were different to mine. His float was a porcupine quill and his line was nylon but the most noticeable difference was in the hooks which, compared to those on my line, were tiny. He also used maggots as bait and, sometimes, hemp.

I couldn't afford maggots, which could be purchased in 'The Budgie Shop', a pet store in Stroud Green Road not too far from the park, but I was able to run to a packet of size 14 hooks, already tied on to what looked like nylon. It was in fact catgut, which proved a nightmare in its own right. Springy and stiff, it wanted to remain in the tight coils that it left the packet in, at least for the first couple of hours fishing. It was only when Old Joe told me that it needed soaking in warm water overnight before use that I realised it wasn't nylon.

Eventually, I added 50 yards of nylon to the green braided line on my reel and that meant I no longer needed to buy hooks already tied: I could now tie my own directly on the end of my 'proper' line.

Until now I hadn't caught a single fish but I'd seen Old Joe catch both roach and perch and could easily tell one from the other; the perch with its bold stripes and 'poisonous' spines. Of course they are not poisonous at all but it's much more fun believing that they are. Armed with my nylon line and the correct size in hooks it was bound to happen soon, but my rod was still much shorter than Old Joe's and I couldn't fish out far enough, restricted as I was by the railings. So, one day whilst feeling both brave and athletic, I climbed over them and could then drop my baited hook twice as far out as before.

My worm hadn't been on the bottom for long – Old Joe told me that you HAD to fish on the bottom and showed me where I had to put my float on the line to achieve that – when the float began to move. It didn't go under – the buoyancy in that celluloid bulb was probably too much for the immature perch that was towing it – but it was moving of its own volition for the first time.

Old Joe had told me to wait until it went under, which meant that I had to set off in pursuit. About 2 yards up the bank the float bobbed almost under and, unable to constrain myself any further, I struck as hard and as far as I could. A perch, all of 4 inches long, flew from the water on to the bank. I dropped the rod and rushed to the fish, flapping on the grass. I unhooked the fish, avoiding the spines, and took it to show Old Joe. He congratulated me on my efforts but warned me to watch out for 'Rubberneck', the 'Parkie'.

I had encountered Rubberneck before. He was nicknamed thus because he had a deformity that thrust his head forward, exposing a large expanse between his brown uniform shirt collar and matching trilby hat. He didn't like many people, judging by his demeanour, and especially didn't like kids. They were trouble and whether his duties were walking round with the pointed stick used for spearing rubbish, calling for number nine to: "… come in, your time is up" from the landing stage or simply patrolling, if you were a kid then you had to behave or: "… you'll feel the weight of the back of my hand."

One thing we could do was run away because there was no way 'Ole Rubber' was going to catch us if we did but it was impossible to run from the 'wrong' side of the railings.

After a while I got the hang of catching fish from the lake but still only perch and never more than five in a day. I'd still not managed a roach BUT I'd bought a new float. This was a professionally made creation with a cork body at the bottom end and a cane stem, with a red top encircled by black painted hoops. I'd got it from a new tackle shop I'd found, in Holloway Road. I discovered it by sheer fluke as I wanted a model aircraft kit – for what reason I have not the first clue as I was then, and am still now, totally incapable of creating, constructing, or even simply assembling anything to resemble anything like what it should be. I've never visited IKEA and I doubt I ever will because of this affliction.

But, while I was looking at the balsa Spitfires and Hurricanes and plastic replica Flying Fortresses, I noticed, at the far end of the shop, some fishing rods. Closer inspection revealed a Pandora's Box of legers, aluminium boxes the size and shape of small match boxes that contained split shot, packets of hooks and, most enticing of all, floats.

Keith Arthur

There has never been a truer word spoken: floats catch far more anglers than they do fish. I have hundreds, maybe more, but in 1954 I had just the one, a situation that needed rectifying.

All thoughts of balsa cement and squadrons of aircraft suspended from my bedroom ceiling disappeared as I could see red tops standing proud of the surface of Finsbury Park Lake before bobbing a couple of times then going under with an almost audible 'plop' as a fish ate my worm. I had to have one and the one I chose was as described above.

I also had enough left from my pocket money that I so nearly wasted on an Airfix kit to buy a small bait box and a tannersworth (2.5p) of gentles, the old name for maggots, as well as a little box of mixed split shot.

I couldn't wait to get to the park and set up my rod. The float took sufficient shot to enable me to cast it a VERY long way, almost to the island. The only problem was it took *so* many that my supply was exhausted before I could make it achieve the inertia required to sit up straight, with that evocative red top standing proud of the water. So it laid flat on the surface.

With maggots on the hook I was extremely confident of catching roach, those beautiful, silver fish whose scales gleamed with blue tones which set off the scarlet fins.

Identifying a bite may have proved a problem but I soon discovered that, with the float horizontal on the water, the bites were 'runs', the float moving along the surface, struggling to stand up as even the swimming ability of the fish couldn't force it to stand up straight and I caught roach.

We had a close season to abide by in those days and that three months had to be filled. I was quite keen on trainspotting – my Uncle Cliff worked on the railway – and Finsbury Park Station, just one stop from Kings Cross, enabled me to 'cop' a few engines, including most of the famous 'Streaks',

The best excuse for loafing in the countryside

as we called them, of which Mallard was probably the most famous example, having broken the world railway speed record. It seemed incongruous that such a famous engine could pull ordinary people along in standard carriages; a bit like a Derby-winning racehorse pulling a cart.

The boating lake wasn't the only water in Finsbury Park: the New River, dug in the 17th century to carry water from the River Lea near Hertford through the Lea Valley into the reservoir chains, was situated at the far, Haringey, end of the park. It ran crystal clear with fronds of *ranunculus* swaying in the current. Standing on the bridge it was possible to see roach hiding in the shade or darting in and out of the weed to intercept food items carried in the flow.

Fishing was very much forbidden, the banks being patrolled by Metropolitan Water Board uniformed guards, accompanied by VERY large German Shepherd dogs. Anyone caught on the banks was in big trouble. Standing on the bridge was OK though, as long as you obviously weren't fishing.

By now several of the other youngsters that lived on the same road as me went fishing, possibly because I'd told them, during games of street football and cricket, how exciting it was. They also knew to beware of Rubberneck because he terrorised anyone breaking any of the park rules, such as playing football on the red cinder pitch or, worse still, the grass pitches!

Paul, Michael and Peter had fished in the lake with me and stood on the New River Bridge, admiring the roach. What we had to do was catch some of them. No casting was involved, so we didn't need a rod; no winding in was involved, so we didn't need a reel; we could fish directly under the bridge. Floats were difficult but matchsticks worked OK, not that it mattered much because we could watch the fish take the bait – and that was our biggest problem: getting caught with anything resembling bait would result in the wrath of Rubberneck.

We could make the fish eat bread, simply pull a little crumb from a crust left from a loaf – no 'cut' bread in those days and bread was bought, or delivered by the horse-drawn baker's van, daily – roll it into a pellet-shape and drop it in. Several roach would attack it almost instantly. Being caught in possession of bread wouldn't be an issue, being caught with line, hooks and matches wouldn't be an issue but being caught with a combination of all four could well be a clump-round-the-ear from the back of Ole Rubber's hand offence.

Then one of us, I don't know who, had a brainwave: cigarette papers! By chewing two Rizla Reds into a pulp they could be made to stay on the hook long enough to catch a roach and how could Rubberneck equate fag papers with bait?

For weeks we took turns-eachers to catch roach, big in our terms at 8 or 9 inches long, maybe 4 to 6 ounces, while the others stood lookout, watching for Rubberneck. I even took to travelling the mile or so up Seven Sisters Road to the park on my roller skates: iron-wheeled monsters that clamped on to my good, school shoes. When fishing the lake they helped by making me that couple of inches taller, handy for fishing over the railings. The mistake I made was using them on another escapade to the New River.

The shortcut from lake to river was down Kite Hill, a steeply sloping grass area where kite-flyers could reach good downhill speed to get their contraptions into the air. A tarmac path wound its way between the grass, enabling mums to push their children in prams. I'd seen daredevils on their skates, crouching on their haunches to reduce wind resistance and thought I'd give it a try.

Rizlas, matches and spool of line, hook attached, in pocket, I set off. The acceleration was slow but gradually increased to a speed I'd never before achieved. In fact the problem was could I stop at the bottom, where the perimeter road ran, carrying traffic that, in those days, was allowed to circumnavigate the park.

A speedy decision, in more ways than one, had to be arrived at. The options were dive onto the grass or simply sit down: I chose the latter.

It is the closest I have ever been to knocking myself out, as well as taking the backside out of my short trousers. I at least managed to maintain some dignity by not crying but it didn't half smart! It smarted even more when I got home: school trousers didn't come cheaply and I was treated to slapped legs for my pains, despite pleas for sympathy. I didn't get to fish either.

In all the times I fished the lake as a lad I never caught more than five fish and they were never all roach but many years later, when I was a regular match angler and had emigrated to south of the Thames, I decided it was time to go back to my angling roots.

I'd heard that one end of the lake had been separated from the remainder by a boom, with a gate installed to allow anglers behind the fence to fish in peace from rowing boats. The story was that tench had been stocked, adding to the roach and perch I remembered from my schooldays.

There were still plenty of youngsters fishing, albeit with superior tackle to that which I'd used 20 years previously. I felt slightly out of place with a continental-style tackle box with drawers full of tackle as well as a match rod and closed-face reel. It would certainly have raised one of Old Joe's impressively bushy eyebrows.

I sat in one of the few available swims and tackled up, feeling the glances of the regulars as I threaded the line, much thinner than I used years before, and set a waggler float on the line. I plumbed the depth in a clear spot between the weed, something that was also new from the old days.

Throwing in a couple of handfuls of hempseed and casters, I flicked the float on top of them and sat back to wait. It didn't take long for it to disappear, the gentle strike being met with the splashing fight of a roach.

Two more redfins followed before a much more serious resistance indicated I'd contacted one of the 'new' tench. It may have been a pound or so in weight but tench were rare enough in my angling CV to be well worth a tingle of excitement.

A couple of the youngsters came up to admire it, asking what bait I'd caught it on and, just as I'd probably done many years before, asking if I had any to spare. I shared out most of the casters and hemp that I had with me, retaining just enough for another hour's fishing.

I recall losing another tench when it made the sanctuary of the Canadian pondweed, transferring the hook, as fish somehow manage to, into a stem of weed. Another roach came to the net before my time available came to a close.

The results of my couple of hours fishing were four roach and that beautiful, green jewel of a tench. Still I hadn't broken the bogey number of five and they weren't all roach either. It was well worth going back though.

Finsbury Park became a rundown facility in the 1970s but huge investment from the Heritage Lottery Fund and careful planning has restored the park to what it was originally planned for: some 'lungs for the Metropolis'. The Environment Agency gave £20,000 for development of fish stocks and angling platforms, including dedicated swims for disabled anglers. Maybe, one day, I'll make another visit.

Hampstead

Hampstead Heath was more like 'the country', with rolling grassland, copses – and corpses too! – along with stacks of wildlife, only missing large mammals; domesticated or otherwise. The attraction for me, of course, was the water: not only did it contain fish but frogs, toads, newts and the ensuing tadpoles, all adding to the allure.

Although I visited, and fished in, all of the ponds, including those where angling was never allowed, most of my activities were conducted at the Parliament Hill Fields end: 'Parly' we called it. Getting there involved a bus ride and then some walking, much easier on the way there as it was downhill, from Highgate Village where the 611 trolleybus, that eventually became the 271 Routemaster when the old electric buses hung up their pantographs, turned round ready for the return journey to Moorgate.

I joined the bus near the Nag's Head, the junction of Holloway and Seven Sisters Road, by the old Gaumont Cinema on the corner of Tufnell Park. The interesting bit started at the other end because the stop was outside Grodzinski's, a Jewish bakery and cake shop that sold 'cheesecake'. I saw it in the window many times but wasn't tempted. Although I adored cheese – and it is still my major calorific downfall to this day – I didn't fancy it made into cakes, which came as fruit or Madeira in my house. Cheese should be strong enough to 'make your teeth itch' was how I described it to my grandmother, and my tastes haven't changed one bit except that I now appreciate cheesecake for what it is – and Grodzinski's is probably still the best.

The walk from the bus stop to Parly was past some big houses along a tree-lined road, downhill most of the way, until Merton Lane which led directly to the ponds. This was – and may still be – notorious for late evening activity in parked cars, something I wasn't to learn about for many years. Schoolboy rumours made me chuckle though, and I would hurry past should I hear the creak of suspension. I was probably hurrying anyway because if Parly, and the Heath as a whole, isn't haunted, then it must be pretty darn close, as well as susceptible to UFO activity.

Once through the entrance at the bottom of Merton Lane the decision had to be taken about which pond to fish because there were four... four legal anyway, plus the 'Ladies' Swimming Pool' about which all sorts of tales were told, not only of plentiful stocks of big fish but also what might be intercepted sunbathing in the long grass surrounding it. Again, I was way too young to know...

All of these ponds are formed from the River Fleet, which rises on the Heath and flows towards the Thames, eventually joining the great river close to Fleet Street.

The first on the right was known as the One-Sider. Like many of its type, when a river or stream is dammed, the pond is V-shaped, with the wider end available for fishing. Fences on either side prevented entry – at the far end began the mystery of the Ladies' Swimmer! A manhole-covered drain at the furthest end of the fishable bank carried the water down to the next in line; the Boating Pond.

Elliptical in shape, this piece of water was used for model boating but it was also great for fishing and, apparently, still is today. The banks were artificial, shored up with concrete and girders to allow the boaters access to enough depth of water to float their boat.

Years after I first ventured down Merton Lane, one of those model boat enthusiasts provided a corpse when, having dived in to retrieve a becalmed craft, he failed to resurface. It took frogmen two days to find the body and, in times when that stretchy plastic tape isn't spread round everywhere that someone breaks a toenail, it was recovered right next to where my pal Bill was fishing. They asked him to turn his transistor radio off 'in respect'.

Bill also had a 'happening' one night whilst fishing the pond. On the far bank, opposite Millfield Lane, a hill rises away from the water. Bill is a couple of years older than me and enjoyed night fishing, something that has never appealed; maybe this experience, related to me soon after it happened, is why.

Bill was fishing with his umbrella set to stop the cool breeze rolling down the hill when, at about 2am, his hair stood on end. It was one of those "should I look round?" moments but Bill, being braver than I would ever be, peered round the umbrella to see a bright, glowing half-moon of light, sitting atop the hill. No vehicles were allowed anywhere near and there was no sound. He said the light lifted off the ground then went out. He still asserts, to this day, that it could only have been a flying saucer. Night fishing? Are you MAD?

At the southern end a drain allowed what there was of the river, a mere trickle but this was a waterway in its infancy stage, to tumble into the Swimming Pond. This was the men's swimmer and fishing was allowed on three of the four sides; the fourth being reserved for swimming and diving. A huge diving board, possibly approaching the Olympic height of 10 metres, dominated that bank and the area close to the board was the target for anglers legering for the bream that lived there. Every so often we'd see carp around it too but they were uncatchable, certainly for 'normal' people fishing there, although I remember Terry Penn hooking a big fish one day that simply kept going, breaking his line. The banks at either end were piled but the side opposite the diving boards were natural, with large rush beds interspersed with cut-out swims where anglers fished.

The final pond in the chain was the Mud Pond, so named because it had natural, unmade banks that were bloomin' muddy and the cause of many a ticking off for me when I arrived home wearing some of the mud. Almost circular, possibly two-thirds of the pool was fishable with the roadside bank being fenced off and full of dense vegetation. It was very shallow and the water level fluctuated depending on rainfall and how much could be spared from the pools above. It was my favourite and I developed quite a good technique and, if I'd known, could have invented a bait that became famous, one of the most famous, for match anglers, in later years.

Across the Heath proper were the Red Arches, home to massive bream, pike and tench, allegedly, where I never had a single bite and where even someone who fished it quite regularly described it as: "… a bite-a-year" water. Further on, the Vale of Health Pond, another shallow, bowl-like area of water, rested next to the famous village on the Heath of the same name. I actually caught a couple of roach there once, when trying for the big bream legend it contained but it was such a long walk, it was a rare excursion.

My first efforts were on the Boating Pond, mostly because I could cast to water deep enough, where I couldn't see the bottom, but also because by careful searching, perch could be found sticking their noses out from under the girders and an adroitly-twitched worm could usually entice one to have a nibble. No rod was needed for this tactic, so my two-piece cane with plastic reel, was laid across the path while I held the float, the worm suspended about 2 feet beneath.

I had a big can at the time: what its original use was I have no clue but it was probably 18 inches long, a foot across and similarly deep. There was a single hole, just big enough for my hand to enter, in the centre of the top and a hinged lid covered the hole. It was perfect for not only retaining any captures but also taking them home to keep in a goldfish bowl. None of them lasted more than a week or so and even when my father bought me a small aquarium it was the same so I stopped taking trophies at a fairly young age.

Perch are magnificent fish for youngsters to catch. They 'fight' far heavier than their weight, their large mouth makes them susceptible to even the most massive hook likely to be used and they LOVE worms, which of course are free and readily available to anyone with a garden and spade: we had both!

Whilst fishing the boater, I could see that many more proper fishermen, with gear like Old Joe, preferred the One-Sider. Not many were that happy to tell youngsters what they'd caught as the question following: "Had any luck mister?" was likely to be: "Got any spare…?" then select from maggots, bread, hooks, weights, line – you get the picture. I was intrigued as to why they'd want to sit there apparently catching not much whilst I could catch perch, still only a maximum of five, in the very next pool. I had to investigate. I didn't have to wait long, and the reason was roach and bream.

The roach, like those at Finsbury Park, had a penchant for hempseed and, to me at least, looked massive: I'm certain some of them must have been pounders. The bream were even bigger and they were falling to a mystery bait: paste. One of the old boys prepared to entertain a youngster told me that paste made from a flour and water dough, mixed with custard powder, was the favourite so on my next visit I was suitably armed. Standing on the drainhole swim, with my porcupine float now used for its intended purpose, I moulded some of the sticky, yellow goo around my hook, cast out trying to reach where the bigger fish *surely* must be and watched as the paste sailed out precisely where intended but my float didn't follow, the paste was simply flying off the hook. After some trial and error, I found that a gentle, underarm swing could put the bait far enough out and keep it on the hook.

The first bite was exciting, even more so when it resulted in my first ever bream. Not the slab-sided dustbin lid that I hoped for but beguiling in its soft silveriness and almost two-dimensional appearance. The trouble was I had to throw it back because it wouldn't fit in my tin; the hole was too small.

One thing that did fit was frogs and when no one was fishing, because of the close season, there were tadpoles and frogs to be harvested from the One-Sider. All I had to do was climb the fence and search the marshy sides. My mum had bought me a new jacket, a windcheater she called it, that zipped up the front and, of course, I had to wear it on my frog safari.

The tin came in very handy because I could stand on it to assist in climbing over the iron railings, with points on the top that were used to protect the ides of the pond. Not being naturally designed for a life of climbing, disaster struck when my foot slipped and I fell, tearing the sleeve of my windcheater from elbow to armpit.

In floods of tears, knowing how hard mum and dad had to work to buy anything, and fearing a bloody good hiding (which I'd never had and never got but always feared) I left the tin and headed for the bus home. Once onboard a lady asked if my knee was OK as I was still blubbing. I'd not even noticed a scimitar-shaped gash, directly below my patella, which had bled copiously down my socks. Oh no; TWO reasons for that good hiding but,

The best excuse for loafing in the countryside

maybe, sufficient sympathy to preclude either. I still have the scar on my knee as a memory.

The Swimming Pond was a tougher nut to crack as the shallow, natural bank was difficult for me to float fish, having only the short rod and miniature centrepin reel. In fact I told my dad that I 'needed' a new rod and he came home with something of which I had never seen the like before, nor since. It had an excellent-looking 'starback' reel, made of walnut with the brass star frame on the back. Unfortunately it was loaded with thick, green, braided line, strong enough to moor ships. The rod itself was no more than 2 feet 6 inches long but curved into a semi-circle with two coils, as in a spring, directly above the reel. He said it was for ice fishing – at Hampstead? I wish I still had it today as I feel sure a museum somewhere is desperately seeking one just like it.

The sides of the swimmer were slightly different though and even a fairly short cast found enough water to catch fish, mostly roach if I could run to maggots as bait, or perch if I dug worms from the garden. Some anglers were catching bream here by legering, something I'd never tried so, on my next visit to the tackle shop, I bought some leger weights. Two types were available: coffins or bullets, both drilled through the centre allowing the line to be threaded through.

When using a float, bites were quite easy to detect: the fish would swim away and the float would follow, but legering was different: there was nothing to see! The answer was a 'dough bobbin'. A pellet of dough, which of course doubled up as paste bait, would be squeezed on to the line between the reel and the first ring on the rod. The weight of the bobbin tightened the line and when a bite happened the line would tighten (usually) or slacken (rarely) and the bobbin would rise or fall accordingly.

Keith Arthur

It didn't take me long to lose my new weights, hooking some unseen snag that had turned into a monster fish by the time I arrived home, which was also the excuse for having to use the doorbell rather than my own key. I'd replaced the lost weights with my front door keys and lost those too! I didn't leger much after that.

By the time I'd discovered the Mud Pond I had a bike, even if it meant wheeling it up most of Highgate Hill, and a better rod and reel. This had been purchased with my wages, 14 shillings (70p) a week from a paper round and my choirboy fee of a guinea a month from St George's Church in Tufnell Park.

The great thing about the Mud Pond – apart from the mud – was that the roach could be seen, often boiling on the surface when maggots were thrown in. My maggots were now coming from a real tackle shop that sold just fishing tackle: Whaley's in Hornsey Road and if I went late in the day I could help myself to chrysalis from the top of the maggot buckets. I noticed that the lighter-coloured ones sunk while the darker, shinier versions floated and the roach simply adored those.

Normal floats, such as the porcupine quills I still used, made the bait sink because of the required weights but by looping a spent matchstick on to the line, the bait would remain floating. I was catching a lot more than five fish now, sometimes even 20 or 30 before my paper round, especially after I found 'the back way' into the Mud Pond, which skirted Highgate Hill.

When I tried the lighter coloured chrysalis and found they sunk, I caught bigger roach. I even picked them out and used them under my 'normal' float tackle and caught roach from the swimmer too. This could have been the birth of 'caster' fishing, made famous a few years down the line by Leigh, Lancashire's two most famous anglers: Benny Ashurst and his son Kevin who caught bigger than average roach from the canal using them, ultimately taking them to Nottingham's River Trent in the mid-60s and rewriting the match fishing history books.

Like I had at Finsbury Park, many years later I went back and revisited the Boating Pond. It looked so much smaller than I remembered it – but bigger than the Mud Pond which looked like a giant puddle – and it now had quite prolific weedbeds. Most of the anglers present were carp fishing too, with two-rod set ups and electric bite alarms.

I sat on the bank with UFO Hill behind me and fished a waggler past the weed, feeding casters and hemp. It didn't take long for my float to dip, the resulting strike being met by a much fiercer resistance than I was expecting. After a brief interlude of in-the-weed-out-the-weed, I slid a beautiful, green-scaled, red-eyed tench over the landing net. I was amazed! Tench were legendary creatures of Parly in my schooldays, inhabiting the Red Arches (officially known as Viaduct Pond) but rarely, if ever, encountered by anglers. Yet I'd caught one, virtually first cast, on my return.

Half an hour later, with a few decent roach in between, I had another, then one of the carp anglers strolled round from the small landing stage at the Swimming Pond end and shattered the illusion.

"Just tench mate?" he said.

"Yes, two tench, decent fish too and a few nice roach," I responded.

"Drive us potty, bleedin' things. They stuck some in here a few years ago and they've bred like rabbits. Can hardly keep a bait in the water some days. The carp are hard enough to catch as it is."

That must have been 20 years ago and I understand that tench and good bream too still drive the carpers 'potty' but if I'd have been able to catch just one of those green beauties when I was 10 or 11, who knows? I may have taken an entirely different path in angling, rather than becoming infatuated with competitive fishing and winning matches.

Keith Arthur

The River Lea Navigation

Until now all my fishing had been on lakes: it was time to investigate rivers. My dad worked in Tottenham, behind White Hart Lane, the home of Tottenham Hotspur football club. I inherited my love of Arsenal from him, so it must have cut him to the quick during the fallow years at Highbury from 1954 to 1970 when Spurs won the Double and three FA Cups whilst our team stumbled from crisis to disaster.

He was a toolmaker at a company that backed on to the railway and often worked seven days a week, for the overtime. Part of his work involved making things such as Lone Star toy guns, so I was rarely short of weapons when the Indians hit Axminster Road. The front of the factory looked out on to a grass playing field and ultimately the River Lea Navigation. Now there is a bypass in between but then it was simply a case of walking across the bridge over the Black Ditch, as the Pymmes Brook was known, to the canalised river, directly upstream of Stonebridge Lock.

We had no family car but dad and I both had bikes and he rode the five miles to work each day. With no traffic at all on Sundays, if he was working, I'd occasionally be allowed to follow him and either watch the trains, collecting the numbers of engines that went from Liverpool Street north and east rather than those I was used to at Finsbury Park that only went north. One day I walked across to the river and saw a man fishing so the next time I was allowed to 'go to work' with dad, I tied my trusty cane rod to the handlebars and with a Gale's honey jar filled with worms I'd dug from the garden – having beaten the chickens he kept to them – I set off across the grass. This was more like countryside!

Being Sunday there was no river traffic – pleasure boating on canals back then would have been laughed at as the Lea Navigation was a truly commercial waterway, carrying timber from the Thames docks to the furniture factories that lined the banks – and the water was still, making fishing quite simple. Except that I couldn't catch anything.

The man was there again, sitting on a fold-up stool and holding a longer rod. I asked him the usual "Had any luck?" question, getting the standard reply of "Not much." He had a tub of maggots so, in best schoolboy nuisance tradition I begged a few and dropped them in with my worms. Eventually I had a bite, before the 12.30pm curfew I'd been given as we had to be home for Sunday dinner, and landed a beautiful silver torpedo. I asked the man what it was, he replied that it was: "… a dace, and a nice one." Nice one? It was a blinking excellent one!

I toddled back across the field when I heard dad calling – I am rarely early or even on time on my return from fishing to this very day – and told him of my success. Pedalling home seemed easier than usual.

Travelling to Stonebridge Lock by public transport wasn't that easy from home but a bus to Manor House – they almost all went that far – followed by a 623 trolleybus to Tottenham Hale put me right on the bank. The bus actually stopped right outside the old Harris Lebus furniture factory and little did I know that a few years down the line I'd be selling their bedroom suites!

Tottenham Lock looked very different to Stonebridge, despite it being less than a mile away. Barges were mostly towed by horses then and at Tottenham, fishing was from the towpath bank, built up so the horses had traction. Many times I have been reminded of the far bank when watching *The Simpsons* as it was mostly taken up by a tyre dump, just like Springfield's finest.

Below the lock, the Black Ditch poured in to the canal, whilst on the opposite bank the Old Lea, the original course of the river, flowed in. The water here bubbled with horrible gases and no one ever considered fishing there. The Black Ditch water could easily be seen colouring the brown-stained canal water. Some days the Black Ditch was black, the other days it ran crystal clear and it took a couple of years for me to find out why: further up the canal from Stonebridge stood a massive gasworks which burned coal to create the gas. When it rained the coal dust washed into the Pymmes Brook, turning it into the Black Ditch!

As I walked along the towpath for the first time I noticed some small areas of 'natural' bank in front of the piled part. I called them The Islands and as I could sit closer to the water, they were the chosen spots. The very best part about fishing there was when a horse pulled a barge past: the dipping, swaying rope would pass directly over my head, whereas if I'd sat on the top, I had two choices: lay flat on the bank or take all my kit back behind the horse's path.

The worst part came when, for some reason, a horse stopped behind me. The impulsion of the barge would then keep it moving, slackening the rope. The helmsman on the barge would have to run to the front and unhook the rope or else the barge could drag the unfortunate horse into the drink. I never saw that happen but had some hairy moments when two barges and two horses came together in front of me. The way that the mighty animals worked in harmony with the driver, who in turn worked as a team with the helmsman must have been a joy to behold although, to be quite honest, I was more concerned with it spoiling my fishing.

Having had success with my dace at Stonebridge I expected more of the same but my main captures were yet another new species: the gudgeon. There were plenty of them and I became obsessive about counting them and to this day I remember quite clearly my best-ever day there when I had 129 fish: 108 gudgeon, 11 bleak (another variety I first encountered on the Lea) six roach and four dace.

On another occasion I actually caught a bream, then another. Only tiny, maybe 6 inches or so long, they were 'rareys', our name for anything less than usual. Rumour had it they'd been stocked when a van carrying them to Walthamstow Reservoirs, less than half a mile away, conked out and they tipped the fish into the nearest water.

We all believed it but it would probably have been easier to push the van the remaining couple of hundred yards and dump them in the Coppermill Stream, the branch of the New River that fed the reservoirs, or tip them downstream of the lock, where the Black Ditch and Old Lea converged with the canal. I guess what really happened was that there were *proper* bream present and they had a successful spawning, an event that, in my experience, happens less than one year in 10 in most waters.

As I grew older I was allowed more independence so I would ride my bike to Tottenham on my own. It didn't last that long though as my excuse for being late was always the long hill-climb from Ward's Corner at Tottenham to Woodbury Down. I was told to take the bus and when that too failed, I was banned completely from fishing. What I had to do was to find a way around the ban.

Around this time my passion for Arsenal FC (THE Arsenal, the only club acknowledged by the definite article THE) was flourishing and I was going to Highbury for the home games – every other Saturday – and fishing on alternate weekends. Being banned from fishing meant I had to stop so, when Arsenal were away, I went to Spurs instead, to support the opposition, no matter who. Or at least, that's what I told my folks. What really happened was that my pal Peter, who lived a dozen or so houses away with his parents was a year older than me and considered quite responsible by my dad so they didn't mind me lending him my tackle, as I couldn't use it. Of course he had his own gear and we used to fish together, at Stonebridge behind Spurs' ground, going by public transport so I'd have the ticket to prove I'd been there. Easy stuff!

It also meant I didn't have to be home by any time earlier than 5.30 – 6pm as the games all kicked off at 3pm and ended at 4.45 or so. We'd fish until the game was over and by the time we got home, the later editions of the *London Evening News* would be out with the results in. What a doddle!!

One week we were even luckier: Spurs were at home to Sunderland and we'd counted the roars and groans of the crowd, a decent barometer of goal action but we were a little later than usual packing up. As we walked across the green towards the level crossing at Northumberland Park Station, a Spurs fan walked past us. He told us the score was 2-2 and gave us a brief précis of the game, including how Sunderland's star Len Shackleton had scored the equaliser. Now we could save the time of checking the score in the paper.

It must have been 6.30pm when I strolled in, apologising for being half an hour late but the crowd had been so big that leaving the stadium had been terrible. Dad asked me the score and I told him what the fan had told me.

"Oh, really" he said. "Sounds like a great game, especially with that late goal. I suppose everyone stayed right to the end because of it, you included."

"Yeah, right to the end, that's why we're so bloomin' late."

Keith Arthur

The resulting clip round the lughole was accompanied by the news that Spurs had actually scored the winner with the final kick of the game. The 'fan' had obviously left in disgust when the Mackems equalised. Banned and grounded, before the term was even invented!

Eventually I was allowed back out and began investigating the Lea further afield. I'd ride my bike to Tottenham Lock or, occasionally, Stonebridge, then follow the towpath north until I didn't fancy the pedal home. I found some great spots too.

The towpath side above Stonebridge was deeper than the bank I usually fished from dad's work days and I caught some roach that must have been 8 or 9 inches long, maybe weighing 6 ounces although to me they were the pounders I'd read about in dad's *Daily Mirror*, in the Mr Crabtree comic strip. I also caught what I thought was my first ever catfish. We had the usual fish bowl at home with two goldfish and a small catfish. It had whiskers around its mouth and so did the small specimen I'd caught. My pet was almost black in colour but the one I caught was mottled and dotted – maybe I'd caught a NEW SPECIES! I saved it in my new fish retaining device: the big can from Hampstead had been replaced with an elliptical cylindrical tin that originally housed 'Hacks', the old-fashioned cough sweet from the sweetshop. I'd carefully tied some string around the top so it would hang from my handlebars, in case I had to take any fish away for livebaits – Mr Crabtree found them best for pike fishing.

When another angler walked past and, as ever, enquired about my luck, I showed him my new catfish. I wasn't sure whether to believe him or not when he said it was actually called a stone loach but when he showed me where to look for them, under large stones on the bottom, or old detritus such as bits of wood, I believed him. It's many years since I last saw one, during a winter league match on the River Mole near Boxhill when one was swimming around in my boot prints when I sat on the grass bank paddling my feet.

Pedalling ever-further north, I discovered the big furniture-making centre at Edmonton: not countryside in anyone's imagination. Further on, Pickets Lock then Ponders End and the flour mill stream. Wrights Mill still stands, and still produces high quality flour too, and outside it is the mill pool that drew its water from the Lea to power the millstones. The stream re-enters the main canalised river directly below Ponders End lock but the power has been electric for nearly 100 years. It was still a very good place to fish, mostly for roach, with legends of barbel which, tantalisingly, used to turn up occasionally below Pickets Lock and, as far as I know, still do. None ever turned up there for me.

Brimsdown, with its power station and railway bridge for the small train that ran to the Royal Small Arms Factory, was a great stop for bream. Mossops Creek was used to moor the barges that brought the coal and also took the fly ash away to be dumped, in the North Met Pit at Cheshunt, also famous for its pike.

Mr Crabtree had told me about pike and how to catch them, with livebait being the answer. I knew where to catch those, especially gudgeon, in copious quantities and I had the means of transport for them (Hacks tin). I'd also been told by Mr Whaley at the tackle shop that Boxing Day was the traditional day for pike fishing. So, using my pocket money, I bought a snap tackle, a pike bung and a pilot float: time for some pike action.

I had been told that fishing on Christmas Day was out of the question so on Christmas Eve I was on my bike to Tottenham Lock, Hacks tin on each handlebar, rod strapped to the crossbar, for my livebait catching session.

Keith Arthur

There were no laws about fish movements and, probably, no fish diseases to worry about so moving a few gudgeon was completely fine. I must have caught 30-odd, plus some roach which I returned and a few bleak which we (the regular bunch of kids that fished there) had started 'liberating' into the swirling waters of the Black Ditch as they got on our nerves, intercepting the maggots we intended for roach and dace. Gudgeon at least had uses as livebait.

On arriving home the gudgeon were placed into a galvanised zink bath, probably the one that my sisters and I had been washed in as small children, awaiting their Boxing Day trip.

The North Met was, and still is, a disused gravel pit that, unlike those of today, was dug where the gravel seams were richest. It has a plethora of islands, bays and peninsulas and, in those days, the Loch Ness Monster. This was the pumphouse where the Brimsdown fly ash was pumped from the barges into the pit: two giant black hoses hung from the canal side of the pump and one great, undulating metal pipe entered the water on the pit side. The water in that area was too shallow to fish but directly past the lock-keeper's house was a bay that was much deeper and, being crescent shaped, just the sort of place where Mr Crabtree would seek out 'Freshwater Sharks'.

The old-fashioned pike bungs were difficult to set at any depth greater than a couple of feet, so with a gudgeon impaled through the lips on one hook of the snap tackle and the other hook through its back by the dorsal fin, I made my cast. I'd bought a gag, a primeval device used to hold a pike's jaw wide open so the hooks could be extracted in safety, but I didn't possess a landing net. Although catching a pike was an impossible dream anyway.

I watched my bung, and accompanying pilot float, bob around the bay for an hour or so until I became bored. I'd already learned that throwing in maggots as loose feed, when using them on the hook, attracted fish; maybe the same would apply for gudgeon and pike, after all I had plenty to spare. I know how cruel this sounds but times have changed so much and this was just pure innocence on my part.

Suddenly the bung bobbed, then again, then, just as Mr Crabtree had told me it would in his comic strip, the float slid gently across the water's surface before gradually descending into the depths. A PIKE HAD TAKEN MY BAIT!!!!

Once the bung was out of sight, the pilot float did its job, sliding up the line indicating where the eating action was taking place. Mr Crabtree had suggested that it was best to let the pike run with the bait; it would then turn it and swallow and move off again and this, at the start of the second run, was the optimum time to strike. I get excited even today when I have a pike take my bait so goodness knows how I felt then.

I swept the rod back with all the force I could muster and felt a weight on the other end. The pike swam from side to side a bit, thrashed on the surface showing its mouth full of teeth but what happened could never be described as a fight. I managed to drag the fish onto the bank over some dying reeds and there it was! I inserted the gag, removed the hooks which, miraculously, were still visible, in fact they were just inside the jaw – good old Crabtree – and bashed the pike across the head with a handy lump of wood. Pike were caught to be eaten then and this would be the very first fish I'd ever caught that I would taste.

I suppose the pike must have weighed 5 or 6 pounds so there was far too much for us, even counting my three younger sisters, so the carcass was cut into steaks and the next morning I pedalled to Finsbury Park and gave some to my great-grandfather, who had always showed an interest in my fishing. He was very old, over 90, and when he became ill a year or two later, my grandmother told me he could only eat boiled fish and how much he'd enjoyed eating my pike. That was the only inspiration I needed to catch more gudgeon and pay another visit to that bay on the North Met. I even managed to catch a fish for him, which I delivered fresh on the way home. It was cooked for him and I was told it was the last thing he was able to eat before he passed away. I'm sure it wasn't the pike that was responsible.

He left me £10 in his will specifically to buy some pike tackle and Mr Whaley saw me right with a Sharpe's of Edinburgh 'Scottie' seven foot spinning rod, made from split cane (cost £3/6/6) and an Intrepid Continental reel which was brand new to the market at £3/5/7. So ended 1959.

The one other great memory I have, although it wasn't quite so enjoyable at the time, features a trip to celebrate the New Year. This time a gang of us decided to go to Stanstead Abbots, quite a long way upstream towards Hertford. The place is known as St Margaret's to anglers and directly above the main road bridge, and below the lock, the River Mimram enters the navigation. The object of our trip was the section upstream of the lock known as the Broadwater. The canal widened out here for a hundred yards or so and it held a shoal of bream, allegedly.

It was unlikely they would feed on this occasion because the canal was covered with 2 or 3 inches of ice for 10 feet or so from the bank, leaving a clear channel down the middle. Most of the gang were there when I arrived on the train – steam of course – and had smashed enough ice to fish through. I took a heavy bankstick and tried to break the ice but made no impression. A stroke of genius (I have them occasionally, thank the Lord!) made me stand ON the ice and try and smash it next to the bank. It worked a treat; the ice cracked in a big sheet, tipped up and dumped me into waist-deep water of the extremely chilly variety. Everyone else, rather oddly, found the situation amusing.

Of course suggestions were plentiful, the best coming from Stan Harris, old enough to have a moustache AND to know better, who suggested I ask the lock-keeper for help in drying out. I was wearing two pairs of trousers for warmth, but that wasn't working, and Wellington boots that were full of two pairs of wet socks containing one pair of wet feet which by now I couldn't feel.

The lock-keeper's cottage had a very welcome looking Christmas wreath on the front door, which raised my spirits, and expectations, but my "Happy New Year, I've fallen in" greeting was answered with "Sorry mate, nothing to do with me." It wasn't exactly what I'd hoped for.

The obvious solution was the station, which had a waiting room with a grate usually filled by a roaring fire – only this was New Year's Day which, even before it became a public holiday, was taken off by many commuters, plus it was a Sunday. The grate was empty and the room was bitterly cold so I went outside and bought a newspaper, then ventured on to the tracks and picked up some lumps of coal, dropped by the trains all along the tracks on those days.

Before long a fire was raging not only in the grate but in the hearth as I'd been slightly over-enthusiastic loading it up. My outer trousers and socks were steaming away nicely on the fireguard and I was steaming away nicely in front of it. The idyll was broken by the station foreman bursting in, probably having seen steam AND smoke rising from the chimney. "You can't do that in here!" he said and didn't seem too receptive to my reply that I already had. I also upset him further by refusing to put the fire out and leave, reminding him that as the railways were nationalised, he was a public servant and I was the public, indeed I was a paying customer! I stayed until I was warm and dry, or at least warm and damp, went back to the river to find that only Stan had caught a solitary, tiny roach so, despite the worst possible start, I'd possibly had the best day.

The River Lea

One thing that could be said about the North Met Pit was, despite the Loch Ness Monster and despite the railway line with steam trains snorting and roaring their way past at regular intervals, it was more like the countryside, especially facing away from the pit, across the Lea Navigation, towards Essex. There lay the Seventy Acres Fishery.

Much of the Seventy Acres was covered by a big gravel pit, similar in concept to the North Met, with discreet bays and wide open areas of water but it was what lay beyond that made me cross the white bridge at Cadmore Lane and walk across the marshy ground to the Old River Lea, although 'Old' should read 'Original' as the Lea Navigation usurped the name.

The river was controlled by the Waverley Angling Society, who sold day tickets for 1/6d (7.5p), collected by Dave, the lock-keeper at Cheshunt Lock. I knew Dave because the bay on the North Met where I fished for pike was directly adjacent to the lock-keeper's house where his wife made wonderful rock cakes, and sold them through the kitchen window along with hot cups of tea, freshly brewed in pre-teabag Britain.

Technically, as I was still under 14, I shouldn't have been fishing there as youngsters were banned from the fishery, even if accompanied by an adult, which I never was anyway. But Dave liked me and knew I was as keen as mustard. We also had a bit of a deal going: he didn't have time to get to a tackle shop very often so I used to take an extra pint of hemp and swap it with him for a dollop of his homemade sausagemeat paste, which he trotted down for chub. If I didn't want sausage paste, the deal applied to a rock cake and a cuppa.

The Lea on this section had a good flow, carrying the main river from the outfall of Kings Weir upstream down to Fishers Green and partially back into the Lea Navigation at Waltham Common Lock, with the remainder of the river going via the Relief Channel, built I believe to protect the Royal Small Arms Factory, which was therefore more or less on an island, with the Navigation on the other side. The flow that entered the Navigation at Waltham Common flowed around Rammey Marsh Lock then out again, adding to the flow of the Powdermill Stream, which formed an aquatic barrier from the south.

But it was 'the Waverley' that drew me. The usual route was the 623 to Tottenham Hale then the train, steam engine and all, to Cheshunt. Every station was a temptation to alight and explore because the line ran parallel to the river but I'd found what I considered to be Paradise.

If I wanted to go *really* early, there was a 'worker's special' 659 trolleybus that left the end of Axminster Road shortly before 5am. There was no connection to Tottenham Hale; the 623s didn't run until sensible o'clock, but the worker's 659 terminated at Lower Edmonton station that, happily, provided an alternative means of arriving at Cheshunt on a different rail line. It didn't pass through so many evocative stations as the Tottenham train: no Brimsdown, Enfield Lock, or Ponders End for example, but it got me to Cheshunt, and the Waverley, early. Oh for the days of integrated transport!

Arriving early, in the half light of predawn, I would semi run from the station in Windmill Lane to the towpath, via the 'cattle creep', on to Cadmore Lane Bridge past the Abbey Cross Pit and across the Navigation onto acres of knee-high grass. As the sun rose, directly in my eyes, above the Essex countryside, the marshy field would be shrouded in grey mist. Trees appeared to float on it, 3 feet above the ground and I'd have trouble seeing my Wellington boots but the sun, 93 million miles further distant, was trying to steal my vision.

Every dying nettle and thistle would be joined by spiders' webs, hanging like inverted diamond tiaras under the weight of dew but, despite that beauty which must have made some impression as I can close my eyes and clearly see it now, almost 50 years on, my destination was clear. I could make out the contour of the river by the trees standing sentry along its banks where the mist rose, like steam, from the water that retained some of the previous day's warmth. I am sure that if my games master at school had been able to make the Waverley visible from seven miles away and had pointed me towards it, I may have made a cross-country champion. But all I wanted to do was be first to cast in and catch the chub before they were properly awake.

My split cane spinning rod and Intrepid Continental were ideal for legering, using either a coffin weight in an attempt to hold bottom in the comparatively rapid flow, or a drilled bullet to trundle the bait into a tight corner; beneath an undercut bank or an overhanging bush for example.

Having read Mr Crabtree quite thoroughly by now, I knew *the* bait for chub and barbel was cheese, pretty handy really as it was, and is, my favourite nibble to this day. Accompanying the cheese would be a tin, usually one that had at some time contained cocoa or Ovaltine – dad's bedtime drink, housing a cluster of lobworms dug from the garden.

All this could be carried in a little ex-Army rucksack, along with a sandwich for sustenance, with my rod and landing net handle – I'd invested in a simple bamboo handle, 4 feet long, and a folding circular-framed net with mesh that smelt of the linseed used to treat it.

Late summer was the perfect time for the Waverley: not only did the chub and barbel feed better but I could get there as dawn was breaking and stay late enough to be in deep trouble when I got home.

Following Mr Crabtree's advice still further, I found an alder tree on the inside of a bend where the bank had been undercut by the flow, perfect chub territory. I sat a few feet upstream of the bush and cast so the current would take my drilled bullet and size 8 hook holding the biggest worm I could find in the tin under the overhanging foliage.

I'd legered in still water before (losing keys, remember?) but my dough bobbin kept rising to the rod so I had to rely on watching the rod tip. After a fairly short time I could identify the little tip-taps as the weight bounced over the clean, gravel riverbed but once it reached the dark area under the canopy, close to the roots where I KNEW chub lived, it barely moved until a sharp, downward pull let me know that chub were at home.

Despite that tree looking the perfect location for big chub, I don't remember ever catching one much above a pound or so in weight and mostly those I captured were much smaller.

Downstream of the bend the river straightened for maybe 25 yards and then took yet another turn, this time a complete 'U' bend with the bank on my side fallen away to a gentle sandy/gravely slope. The far bank looked very interesting with all the main flow of the river pushing across, alder trees standing on top of the bank which must have been 5 or 6 feet high. This just had to be Chub Corner!

Instead of worm, I pushed my hook into a cube of Holland's finest Edam and cast out as close to the far side as I dare, a distance of no more than 15 yards or so. Within a very short time the weight had been carried by the current and was closer to my bank than the opposite side. I replaced the circular bullet with a larger coffin weight and recast: that kept it still but not for long.

I had placed my rod in a rest with the tip pointing skywards and the cork handle on the gravel. The first bite pulled the rod tip down so far the handle lifted off the ground! The 'slipping clutch' worked for maybe the first time since I'd owned the reel as the fish tried to get under the far bank – indeed it felt like it had burrowed way under, almost to the greenhouses visible in the distance. The creature on the other end of the line also headed upstream, whereas the chub I'd caught all tried to get under the bank and go downstream.

Eventually the fish subsided and appeared in the shallow margin. It was a barbel and the excitement of the battle and the appearance of this magnificent streamlined torpedo, the colour of an old, brass threepenny bit with four rubbery barbules around its mouth, made me shake with excitement. To this day, whenever I hook a barbel, I suffer precisely the same effect and I've caught a few over the years.

I slipped the landing net under it and laid it in the water's edge while I unhooked the fish, which still had enough power to writhe under my restraining grip. After unhooking, I released the barbel, which swam powerfully back towards its far bank home. Barbel Bend was born!

By the start of the next season I had acquired a new item of tackle: a 'roach pole'. The advert in the angling paper had described it as 16 feet long, made from high quality bamboo with a tip so flexible a knot could be tied in it. Why anyone would want to tie a knot in a fishing rod I don't know but at 18/11d, plus P&P, from Maskells, 346 Uxbridge Road, W9, it was a must-have piece of kit. I'd found a swim on the Waverley where I knew it would be perfect.

Keith Arthur

The old river ran roughly parallel to the Navigation and a few hundred yards above the lock was a cutting that took any excess canal water and ran it into the Lea. This formed a bay where lilies grew – it would have been far too rapid for them on the shallow straights, where it was streamer weed, or the slower deeper water (between Chub Corner and Barbel Bend was this kind of water) and there the main growth was 'cabbages' as we described them; underwater patches of pale green, soft-leaved plants common on most limestone river systems.

Because there was little flow in the bay, the fixed length of line used with a 'pole' would allow me to fish accurately. At this time the Lea had plenty of small fish, including minnows and many saw those as a nuisance. However, it wasn't long before I found them anything but. My single maggot on a size 16 hook was taken by a minnow which, in turn was taken by a big perch. Now I always claimed that perch to be 3 pounds but if I am brutally frank, it may not have been. It was certainly big but I'm not one of those anglers that accurately weigh each and every fish and I didn't carry any scales. But it was big and 3 pounds seemed a fair call at the time.

This piece of good fortune – having the perch take my hooked minnow – led me on two different paths. The first was on the Coppermill Stream at Enfield Lock where the clear, fast-flowing water contained a proliferation of underwater foliage and beds of dark green rush, waving in the current. It also contained minnows in massive abundance. A wire fence ran alongside but, at about waist high, it was quite easy to simply fish over it. I would bait my hook – a slightly larger size 14 – with a maggot, drop the float in with the hook set maybe 2 feet beneath it and walk along the bank, keeping pace with the flow, until I hooked a minnow.

These minnows all lived together in colonies close to the bank where the water was slightly slower than the main stream and when I caught one, I'd simply lift it from the slacker water and deposit it in the fast stuff, still firmly hooked. As soon as the minnow swam down between the waving beds of streamer weed and cabbage, a perch would pounce. Not every time but often enough to make it a very viable method. I was astonished at how very small perch would attack the minnow and even more amazed when I tried an artificial spinner on my rod and reel. It attracted every fish in the river and entire shoals of bleak and small roach and dace would swim after it! I learned a LOT about fish behaviour on the Powdermill Stream, mostly that, like sheep, fish play 'follow the leader'. In later years when fishing for dace in contests I never allowed my float to travel through a shoal of fish for fear of hooking the one at the back: as it wriggled and gyrated, the rest of the shoal would fall in behind it, taking the fish ever-further downstream.

Once I had a paper round I could afford better tackle, a longer 'float rod' and a proper trotting reel, like Mr Crabtree. Mr Whaley didn't have the Rapidex or Trudex as favoured by the anglers I read about each week, but he did have an identical reel marketed by the Edgar Sealey tackle company. The rod, 12 feet long and in three sections, was built from Spanish reed with a 'spliced built cane' tip. It was as stiff as a poker (and about as heavy as an RSJ!) except for the more pliant tip, where the built, otherwise known as split, cane was spliced into the reed about 9 inches from the brass ferrule that connected the top and middle sections.

On my first visit to the Waverley with my new gear I decided to trot down the shallow water above Chub Corner. It had a hard gravel bed with sparse patches of streamer weed.

On the aforementioned straight between Chub Corner and Barbel Bend I learned the art of fishing with hemp. The 'deadly weed' as it has been described over the years, is possibly the source of more myth, legend and general misinformation than any other angling related item, certainly more than any bait including bloodworm. Amongst the better ones are that it grows on the bottom of lakes and rivers where fish eat the plants and become addicted – hooked, I suppose – as hemp is the source of cannabis. That's about as daft as suggesting sailors could become addicts through sucking rope!

It is also impossible to expect a fish to eat anything else once it has tasted the 'forbidden fruit'. That being the case, what did fish do for the three months of the close season, never mind the whole winter period when hemp was considered a waste of time? They certainly seemed to survive.

Dave the bailiff told me about hemp and suggested I try it. The first effort wasn't that good because he didn't tell me I had to cook it. I bought a pint from The Budgie Shop – it is also a bird food and they don't seem to become hippies – and immediately thought they'd sold me the wrong thing because I couldn't get it on the hook, nor could I make it sink when throwing it in as loose feed. It made Dave chuckle when he came for my day ticket money though and he explained it needed boiling for 20 minutes in an old saucepan. Unfortunately we didn't have any old saucepans at home and my first efforts stank the house out as the earthy odour permeated every room.

Necessity being the mother of invention, I found a way to produce perfectly prepared bait with (virtually) zero pong. If you want to try it, there is no patent so go ahead. Put the hemp in a saucepan that won't be used for custard or similar, cover with twice the quantity of water and bring to the boil. As soon as the water starts to bubble properly, put the lid on the pan tightly and switch off the gas, or remove from the heat if electric. Two hours later your bait will be ready.

Recipe over, back to the fishing. Dave advised me to throw in a dozen or so grains each cast and let the float trot down the river. He warned that the bites would be like lightning – he told the truth! – and that I'd miss a lot – correct again – but I'd catch some really good roach – three out of three! However, the stunning thing was that the roach would rise, as a shoal, in the water to intercept the bait almost as soon as it landed. In fact after a couple of hours, I wouldn't even have to feed: just wave my arm in a throwing motion and the fish would come looking; a warning that they see everything! The bites were so fast and the weight of my rod made the strike so slow I had to find a way of hooking the fish and did so by pulling the line instead of lifting the rod. I'd cast in, throw my hemp a couple of feet in front of the float then gently pull the line between the reel and butt ring, keeping it completely tight to the float. The fish hooked themselves most of the time.

On several occasions I'd be playing a good roach, three-quarters of a pound at least, and a perch of similar dimensions would try and eat it! That, together with my experience on the Powdermill Stream with minnows, gave me an idea to catch some of those perch and by casting under the big willow on the far bank of the river, I could catch tiny chub, maybe 3 or 4 inches long, and use those as livebaits. I never caught a perch as large as the one on my pole, but I had a few crackers.

The geography of the area has changed dramatically since the 1950s and 1960s: the marsh has been further excavated for gravel, indeed the entire Seventy Acres is now mostly water and the Old Lea, although still a wonderful fishery, is now a shadow of what it was then, thanks to the building of the Relief Channel and 'improvements' to the course of the river. It is still, though, most definitely countryside and a generally fine place for a spot of organised loafing.

Keith Arthur

The Tamesis

I have used the ancient name for the River Thames, subject of many years' loafing, because it was also the name of the club that introduced me to real competition fishing. It wasn't my first angling club but more of that eventually.

My first exploits on the Old Father came about courtesy of the number 27 bus. The route travelled from Archway, between Upper Holloway and Highgate, to Teddington but on summer weekends went all the way to Hampton Court. The advent of the Red Rover – anywhere on any red bus – weekend ticket for half-a-crown (junior fare, under-14) meant I could make the journey easily and affordably.

I had no interest whatsoever in the famous Royal Palace, indeed I entered through the gates for the first time in 2008 and that was for a meeting concerning angling. What attracted me was the fishing potential.

Opposite the palace is a sloping grass bank that leads down to a flat area ideal for fishing. The stretch is quite short because just a couple of hundred yards below Hampton Court Bridge the river is joined by one of its main tributaries: the River Mole. The spot looked perfect.

I had my trusty split cane rod bought with the money from great-granddad's will, and my Intrepid Continental. I intended to leger as the river looked so vast, float fishing would only allow me to fish what seemed too close to the bank.

I settled in the spot where the two rivers converged and hooked on half a lobworm, casting it into the area where the two flows combined. Nothing happened for a while so I wound in to recast and felt something on the end. It didn't feel like a fish as it wasn't fighting, or even swimming, but a fish it was and a new species to boot!

Only 5 or so inches in length, it was like a piscine pineapple with spines and barbs everywhere. Drably coloured at first glance, closer inspection revealed subtle tones of amber and lilac in a complicated pattern with a proportionately large head. The mouth was where it should be and somewhere within it was my hook but the little varmint wouldn't oblige by opening up, acting like a coward in a dentist's chair.

Eventually I managed to prise open the bottom jaw but could find no sign of the deeply-swallowed hook so I had to use my disgorger, in those days a 6-inch long aluminium rod with a 'V' cut into the tip. By some basic surgery I managed to get my hook back and returned the fish to the water, although its future prospects didn't look the brightest.

Identification was the next step; my 'best shot' being that it must be a cross between a perch and a gudgeon because it had the spines, and then some, of the former and a colouration similar to the latter.

I caught plenty more that day too, I recall 46 in total, plus one good roach (a pound at least I told mum and dad, so probably 8 ounces or so). I couldn't wait to get back for more of the same.

When I arrived back home I told all my mates, who also fished, like most of the youngsters in the 1950s and early 60s, and a repeat visit was arranged. I also found out that the mystery hybrids were in fact 'pope', as they are known in the south of England, the more common name being ruffe, probably because of the way the gills flare on capture looking somewhat similar to the collars worn in the day when Hampton Court was inhabited by the chap who ordered it to be built.

It's a long bus ride from North London to Hampton Court but the journey was filled with the tales of monsters we were going to catch. And this time I had my float rod too. The invasion party included Peter, Paul, Micky and Michael and when we arrived the excitement was palpable.

Obviously we couldn't all fish 'the pope swim' so we fished in a line along the grassy bank opposite the palace. The fishing wasn't great, as I recall, but we had the odd roach and dace, plus some gudgeon but, disappointingly, no sign of the pope. It had been a beautiful, hot summer's day when we arrived but now the sky had darkened and ominous rumbles of thunder could be heard, gradually becoming louder.

Then it was dark enough to see the lightning but, oddly, there was no rain – until we saw a sheet of water travelling down river. The bridge, just a hundred yards or so away, disappeared in the downpour and we scrambled to the top of the bank to shelter under the conker trees – not the wisest option but certainly the driest available.

The noise of the rain on the leaves, the crack as lightning and thunder occurred almost simultaneously made for a deafening chorus but our rods fished on, the floats visibly gleaming red in the gloom.

I don't know who started it but someone shouted: "Micky, your float's gone under, QUICK!!!!!" Micky wasn't the most nimble of kids – he had a shot like a cannonball in our football matches though – and he set off down the grassy slope to hook his fish. Gravity and impulsion then joined forces to provide one of the most entertaining and humorous exhibitions of athleticism I've ever seen. The speed Micky had gathered running down the slope was too much for his braking system and he carried on running – like Roadrunner's Wily Coyote off a cliff – with no ground beneath his feet.

He was already wet but became considerably wetter when he hit the water and stood, chest-deep, in the Thames. There was nothing we could do to help as we were mostly rolling around on the grass in extreme danger of further dampening our undergarments. How he missed landing on one of the rods is a mystery to this day: how he missed the bite is easier to reconcile. It was a damp journey home.

Having tried the 27 to Hampton Court, summer holidays gave us the chance to try it midweek to its usual destination, Teddington Station. The walk from there to the Thames was only a few hundred yards and it had to be worth a go.

The river here was very different, especially the first part which reached down Teddington High Street, then into Ferry Road as it is the main stream from Teddington Weir. A suspension bridge (the swing bridge we called it) crossed the weir stream to the lock cut where the still water looked very fishy indeed.

It wasn't very productive but someone had told me about Ham Pit, where the river is connected by lock gates to a disused sand pit. I eventually discovered that this was the source of Ham River Aggregates, a gravel and sand suppliers who had dug this and several other adjoining pits to supply building materials for the rebuilding of London following the Second World War. Barges would be laden with sand or gravel and travel through the lock gates into the Thames for the downstream voyage to London with just one other lock, at Richmond, to pass through unless the tide was up when special gates used to maintain a navigable depth above Richmond Lock, would be opened allowing free passage.

Keith Arthur

When I found them, most had been filled in with only the one connected to the Thames remaining. Whether it is unique in format is difficult to say but once excavation had ceased and the barges were no longer required to travel through the lock gates connecting to the Thames, the other gate was removed. Now, to this day, when the tide in the river rises, should the level reached be higher than the water in the pit, the gate is forced open and the river fills the lake. Once the flow turns, the gates shut by the same pressure and remain closed. The water level within the pit is never static.

Nowadays it is the home of some very big carp but we found good roach, some bream and our first encounter with roach/bream hybrids. It was also my first experience of night fishing. A group of us, a different group to before with my mate Bill and his brother Dave and a different Dave, set off on Saturday afternoon to fish until Sunday. We had torches, folding stools, food and drink and enough bait to see us through. What we didn't have was shelter or adequate clothing – it's hard to imagine how chilled one can become sitting beside water through even a warm, summer evening. We were so cold we had to start a fire but the twigs and bits of wood we could find, or break off the surrounding hawthorn and elder trees, were wet and simply wouldn't light. Then someone had a brainwave.

At the end of the pit furthest away from the river was a huge building site where a vast number of houses were in various stages of construction. Some of them were in the process of having the roof put on and roof felt burned easily. Dave and Dave took the torches – there was no street lighting and everywhere was totally black – for a recce and came back struggling with a full roll of felt between them. It went onto our smouldering excuse for a fire and was ignited. Boy did that stuff create heat and light but the smoke was choking! Not to worry though, we'd be warm and could see what we were doing with no torches.

The euphoria lasted only for an hour or so until car headlamps appeared on the far side. Fearing, quite correctly, that it was the police: 'Old Bill' where we came from, we kicked the burning roll into the lake where, with mush hissing and steaming, it went out. Old Bill soon turned up beside us asking what was burning but the evidence was long gone. We caught some fish too. Despite the brevity of heat and light from the fire and the fact that torch batteries lasted for a very short time, we were able to see enough to catch some quality roach and bream in the dark by pushing our floats right up the line then swinging our baited hooks into the lake and watching the float hanging under the rod tip. Our bait couldn't have been more than 10 feet or so from the bank, in 2 feet of water or less but darkness was our friend.

I fished the pit many times, once arriving to find someone had fenced it off, with a locked gate at the road end. We had to fish in the cut where the pit joined the river but went next time armed with a set of wire cutters and made our own private door.

Coincidentally I now live less than a mile from the pit but have fished it just once in the near-40 years I've been living in the area.

The rest of the Thames remained a mystery to me until I joined Tamesis in 1963. It was a club set up to fish London Anglers Association (LAA) matches but I'd have an apprenticeship to serve before I had the chance to enter a match, the first part of which was to steward an LAA competition. That entailed walking a designated stretch of river watching the anglers to make sure they didn't break any rules – I was given a booklet with them all in – or to assist should they need to weigh a fish 'in distress' as dead fish didn't count. I was also issued with a metal rule to measure catches as the contests were all fished to strict size limits, fish long enough to be weighed in were known as 'goers' because they could go to the scales. It's amazing that many fish survived as every fish had to be weighed at a central point on the 'section': the length of river chosen for the match was divided into sections, with the total number of anglers spread equally among the sections.

The first section I stewarded was downstream of Maidenhead Railway Bridge, famous for once having the widest and flattest brick arches ever built as well as for the 'sounding arch', which crosses the Thames towpath and produces a wonderful echo. It was, as if you hadn't guessed, designed by Brunel.

I had been instructed to keep a close eye on what was being caught as in LAA matches swims could be chosen rather than as in the rest of the country where anglers had to fish from designated numbered 'pegs', with numbers drawn from a hat. The draw on LAA matches was to decide the 'walk-off' with the angler drawing number 1 walking off, followed in sequence at 10-second intervals. Knowing the best swims was vital to success and I was the team spy!

One angler I'd been told to watch out for was 'Twiggy' who had a new legering method that seemed to produce fish as fast as the traditional Thames float fishing tactics of the day and had the added advantage of catching bonus, big fish, especially barbel.

It didn't take long to find Twiggy, his trademark long hair and blazer and grey flannel trouser 'uniform', covered when necessary by a large gabardine mac, gave the game away. He was fishing on what we called 'The Wall', not far downstream of the railway bridge so I watched him from the start. I didn't learn much though as he would wind in a fish and then dip his keepnet into the water to land it, rather than use a landing net. I simply couldn't get a glimpse of his magic tackle. Houses lined the bank along The Wall section and where they, and the track ended, bushes enclosed the footpath. I went and hid in them.

Soon Twiggy hooked a big fish, obviously a barbel, and as he was fighting the fish I walked up and stood right next to him. There was no escape for his box of tricks now – except there was! Twiggy simply put his rod on the ground and put his foot on it, whilst telling me I was wasting my time as he wasn't going to wind in whilst I was there.

Because Twiggy's secret had such a dramatic effect on the whole of match fishing, and continues to do so up to this day, I will tell the whole story of its 'release' in a later chapter.

I did not get to fish for the Tamesis team in any of the important matches, mostly the LAA Knockout Shield competition, but I won a few minor individual trophies on other LAA matches such as the Thames Championship, Geen Cup, and the Thames and Lea Benevolent events. My main LAA successes came later, with a club I helped form, the story of which is in a later chapter.

Although a small club, with never more than the minimum membership requirement of 12 anglers, Tamesis had some success but didn't win the Knockout Shield in that incarnation. They were up against fearsome opposition at a time when matches were few and far between and the LAA membership was vast, with every North London match angler in it, and a few from south of the river too.

We had a club outing each week there were no matches – and we only had the four above, plus the Shield which only had a six man team and the two big Open events on the Thames, the Southwark Open at Windsor and the Hammersmith Open around Walton. The club only went to Thames venues, unless it was flooded then we went to the River Lea, and we had some great times. Originally we went in a proper 47-seat coach, which cost £8 for the day, including driver and fuel. Fifteen bob each took us as far upstream as Goring! When the price went to £10 we hired a Bedford minibus and driver for £5. It's difficult to imagine that these days.

Occasionally we'd visit a venue where the train was a better choice of transport; one of those being Romney Island at Windsor on the Thames, in the shadow of Windsor Castle. The station is a shorter walk to the river than the car park and it had the added benefit of a station canteen where we could wait after the weigh-in. The staff did the cooking and the apple pie was to die for. After one trip there we had drunk our tea, and eaten our pie when one of our number, Derek Marsh, decided he'd have another piece for the journey. It was sitting on the table when he popped into the loo, a dreadful mistake. Clive Grimshaw, another club-mate, immediately opened his tackle bag and, after lifting the lid off the pie, put a sprinkling of cooked hemp and maggots into the apple. When Derek returned we were all looking the other way, as you can imagine.

Derek decided he couldn't wait for the train before scoffing his second portion and took a big bite. By now, the rest of us were holding our sides from laughing with one hand, the other covering our mouths, imagining it was us with the maggoty pie. Derek, completely unperturbed munched his way through the lot, explaining that the first bit we had must have been old as this new piece was far tastier than the last. Even when we told him the reason for our mirth, he didn't believe us. I suppose it says a lot for the old British Rail canteen grub.

My stay with Tamesis lasted less than three years. They were sticklers for rules and on one outing, to Bourne End on the Thames, I was accused of having two rods set up and ready for use. I'd started off float fishing but changed to a leger rod as sport was slow. The float had been removed from the line, the line itself wound on to the reel but I hadn't taken the rod apart. I was in a very good swim, having walked a long way to the farthest point, opposite Woottens Boatyard where some big chub were known to reside, and I have a feeling to this day that they were worried I'd win the match. At the next meeting I was found guilty and 'suspended' from club activity until the end of the season, six weeks away. I felt like Chuck Connors in the old western TV series *Branded* (you'll need to be old to know that) when he was stripped of his military uniform, even having the buttons cut off, as I handed in my treasured LAA ticket.

I had made some good mates though and found my feet in match fishing so I had yet another excuse for loafing.

Keith Arthur

Teddy and the Big Cod

One of the very best anglers who fished the Thames in the 1960s and 70s was Teddy Barnett. He was a member of the Albatross team, probably the first match fishing 'superteam', at least as far as the London Anglers Association was concerned.

Along with team members such as Bobby Gleed, Bernie Jones, Stan Elkington and Bernie Bristow, they dominated many of the LAA events and even struck out away from the Lower Thames and Lea, entering the Federation of Thames Angling Association Thames Championship, held on the river upstream of Oxford.

Bobby Gleed founded the Thamesley Tackle Company that was amongst the first to produce swimfeeders, certainly the blockend feeder, and produced split shot and leger weights from their East London factory. Bernie Bristow was his general manager.

Bernie Jones helped Bobby set up the firm, while he, along with Freddie French, was a founder of the Glen Insurance Company, one of the largest insurance brokers in North London. Glen Insurance organised one of the biggest angling matches of the year in the 1970s, possibly the first sponsored match as, through their contacts and customers, they gathered a massive list of prizes for the competitors. Pools, in the form of sweepstakes, were still pretty rare and trophies were the usual reward for the winners.

Keith Arthur

The Glen match had prizes though and I well remember Andrew Partridge winning on the River Cam just downstream of Cambridge and collecting a bedroom suite: wardrobe, dressing table and chest of drawers, for his prize. I don't know what position I came in that event, I weighed in a pound or so, but I took home a handbag – for my wife of course.

As for Teddy, well he owned a tackle shop in New North Road, Islington. Since the upward-mobilisation of London N1, I daresay the shop, Vic's Tackle, named for the original owner, is now a bijou café or delicatessen selling olives and sun-dried tomatoes but in the 1960s it was a budding match-angler's dream. In fact Teddy taught me the knot I use for tying spade-end hooks to this very day. He stocked specialised items of fishing tackle, designed for Thames anglers that were unavailable elsewhere: things such as a measuring stick for checking that fish made the size limit and could be counted, or even put into a keepnet.

He always had a good selection of hooks and crow quills, including some he said were from India: far straighter and longer than the standard crow quill, which was more or less the only float used on the Thames back then. If the river was high and flowing fast, it was merely a case of gluing on a cork or, for the *really* dedicated, 'elder pith'. This material was gathered from elder bushes in November, at the end of the growing season, when new shoots died off and were harvested for the very light and extraordinarily buoyant pith that was exposed when the outer skin was removed.

There was far more to Teddy than just match fishing. He loved the River Avon – for some reason known to all as 'The Hampshire Avon' although much of its length runs through Wiltshire and Dorset – and he especially enjoyed sea fishing from boats.

During the close season, those 91 days between March 14th and June 16th when anglers were forbidden to fish for coarse fish, Teddy would make the trip to the Kent coast to fish for cod. Usually this entailed hiring a boat and boatman for the day as the shore fishing wasn't so good after the winter had gone, plus it was essential to be able to cast a long way to find the larger 'spring' cod from the beach; a boat just made it easier to catch some fish.

The cost of the 'charter' depended on the boat: if it had a 'cuddy' where relief from the chill winds could be had, the price would be around £4; open boats were £3. That is for the boat, for the day! The services rendered were very different to those available currently: bait was rarely available, there was no tackle for hire, or loaned out and, as for cups of tea… well!

The first invitation I received to join Teddy on a trip came from my mate Brian, whose parents owned The Old Crown, a big pub opposite St Joseph's Church (Holy Joe's to the locals) and Highgate Cemetery, where the tomb of Karl Marx is situated.

Neither Brian nor I were old enough to drive so we travelled down to meet Teddy on the 611 trolleybus, no mean feat for a 6am start: Dover was a good two hour run from North London, with the City to traverse, and no motorway. Plus we always had to stop for a massive breakfast, the stop on the A2 being The Dunkirk, a true transport café that provided sufficient fuel to stoke the furnace for at least 12 hours for half-a-crown (2/6, or 12p)!

Teddy's car was a Ford Popular; not the original model with the flat back and round nose, but the 'new' version, preceding the Anglia, with a symmetrical appearance of protruding bonnet and boot. Teddy and Brian sat in front, with me in the back seat next to, and holding, our rods.

On every trip I made down the Old Kent Road with Teddy, he would drive over London Bridge as the first commuters were making their way from the station on the south side across to the banks and offices on the north bank.

"There they go, the mice on the treadmill," he'd say, every single time.

Once the Dunkirk was behind us, it would be onward to Dover Harbour, park up (loads of space and all for free!) and find the boat. Our Dover regular boatman was called Johnson; I never heard or knew his first name, he was just 'Skip' as far as we were concerned.

His boat was of the open variety but came at £4 a day because it was berthed in Dover Harbour. We had to climb down a dockside ladder to load the gear on. Unlike today, we each had one rod, one reel and some end tackle, mostly big, lead weights, swivels and hooks: no fancy-dan traces or the like. Our bait, which we had to bring with us, was lugworm. I never heard the word squid used and wouldn't have thought it was available, which didn't matter, as lugworm was plentiful and relatively cheap.

Our lug came from a man in Albert Street, Whitstable who advertised in *Angling Times*. We'd have a couple of hundred each, delivered to Waterloo Station for collection at the price of 10/6 (52p) for each 200, packed in a wooden box lined with newspaper, tied up with hairy string.

After the first trip out with 'Skip' I learned to take an Oxo tin – the trade packaging for those little beef stock cubes – to hide my worms in as Skip also took a rod, but no bait, and fished for his own tea. He wasn't shy on loading up two hooks with half a dozen or so lug, *our* lug, on each hook either!

Skip's boat was a clinker-built affair, a bit like a larger version of the kind I rowed around Finsbury Park Lake, with a diesel inboard engine that had to be coaxed into life by cranking a handle sticking from the box which housed the motor, set amidships. Steering was by a wooden tiller. I never saw a compass used, GPS had not been thought of, echo-sounders (fish finders) and the like were certainly not about, at least not in Skip's boat.

My 'sea rod' was homemade from a fibreglass blank I'd bought, pre-sanded corks glued to the thick end, with sliding reel fittings to hold a bakelite 'starback' centrepin reel. I'd carefully whipped on a set of 'Regalox' rod rings, each with a pink-coloured plastic centre, and a roller guide to the tip. The reel was loaded with 30 pound line.

Brian, with parents as rich as Midas himself to my young eyes, had a 'proper' rod and multiplier reel as, of course, did Teddy: well, he had a tackle shop didn't he?

Skip cranked the putt-putting motor into life, amidst a plume of purple-grey smoke belching from the exhaust, and we made our way at all of 5 knots through the imposing entrance of Dover Harbour.

Not more than 20 minutes into the voyage, Skip, by virtue of lining up some secret marks on the gleaming white cliffs, had us in 'the spot'. The anchor was dropped and, once we had swung round in the tide, the order to lower our baits was given.

It didn't take long for Teddy to draw first blood, a cod of maybe 8 pounds or so coming aboard. Brian and I both winched up 'Channel' whiting of well over 2 pounds each and Skip brought his rod, and our lugworm, into play.

A couple more cod, none to me, and a few whiting later, and the tide died. Maybe for the first time my weight and bait made it all the way down to the bottom and my rod nodded. I set the hook and started to wind for all I was worth. I put maybe 12 yards of line back on the reel when it all went solid. I could feel some life down there but couldn't gain an inch, eventually being forced to pull for a break.

This happened once more and I imagined a massive denizen of the deep engulfing the poor old cod or whiting that I had hooked. Nobody else on the boat had it happen and it's only recently that I realise in all probability I had tangled with the anchor rope as the boat swung about on a slack line during the tide turn. Once the line snapped, the unfortunate, well partially unfortunate as the ultimate bad luck would have been to be boated and eaten, fish could shake its head and free the hook from the anchor warp, swimming away to lose the hook from its lip by some other means.

Skip said that I was wasting my time fishing during the slack and should wait for the flood to begin. All that could be expected during the interim period was dabs.

I wasn't worried what I caught, as long as I caught, plus I could actually use some of my lug, rather than watch Skip feed a bunch of them up his hooks and continue to thread them up his line until he had a foot-long bait.

"How do I catch dabs then Skip?" I enquired. "Small hook, single lugworm," came the reply, so I cut off the huge thing that I had been using, replacing it with a smaller, size 1 hook Teddy said it was, and pushed my solitary worm up the shank.

It had only been down on the bottom for a few seconds when I felt a small bite. "Leave it Boy, let the dog see the rabbit," came Skip's instruction, so I waited until the pulling became more urgent and, somehow, heavier.

I wound the line tight, then struck as fiercely as I dared. "Don't pull its bloody head orf Boy," Skip shouted, but I was more concerned with whatever was trying to pull me over the low side of Skip's boat.

"This is a biggun," I declared, only to be met with the riposte from Teddy: "Not another one of them sharks got yer cod is it?" I knew it wasn't one of the 'monsters' encountered previously because I was continuing to wind in: nothing had stopped me doing so. My rod tip, poker-stiff as it was, could also be seen nodding as the fight continued.

After much grunting and groaning, a shape appeared maybe 25 yards downtide – during the battle the flood had begun – in the murky English

Channel water. It was a cod, and a big fish too. Its mouth was agape, making it ever-more difficult to drag against the increasingly strong tidal flow and, remember, this cod was on a delicate 1/0, fine-wire hook, not one of the forged 4/0 grappling irons we had been using previously.

Later, rather than sooner, the cod was beside the boat and Brian was leaning over the gunwales with the gaff. A single sweep with the gaff handle and the cod was harpooned through the back and dragged into the boat. It looked, and was, massive compared to what had gone before, even though both Brian and Teddy had boated fish close to 10 pounds.

Now the tide was flooding, bites became more regular and as I now knew what it felt like for my lead to hit bottom, I even managed to keep it there long enough to catch a couple more fish, ending the day with two cod and five 'channels'. I had the foresight to take a pillowcase with me to fetch my catch home in – pessimism has never been a weakness for me – and, with the fish stowed in Teddy's boot, we set off for home.

It had been a long day and it wasn't long before Brian and I began that slow, gentle, nodding of the head that signified the start of the 'long blink', which another pal of mine described as the 'car doze'. Teddy woke us up each time with "Oy, you two, no one sleeps in my car while I'm awake!"

Soon we were into the suburbs and the journey became more stop-start – and Brian and I began nodding more in earnest. Suddenly there was a massive BANG, a squeal of brakes and Teddy screaming at someone. Of course we were awake like a shot, Brian half out of the passenger door, and me trying to get out with him: obviously there had been an accident and it sounded like, with Teddy's tone, a rolling-around on the floor was about to ensue.

All that actually happened was Teddy roaring with laughter: he'd wound down his driver's door window, slammed on the brakes and slapped the outside of the door as hard as he could to imitate a coming-together.

"I told you no one sleeps in my car while I'm awake," he said. I certainly never did again.

The rest of the journey was in complete peace, except the barracking of the treadmill-mice on the return journey across London Bridge, the only thing I hadn't thought of was I had to carry my catch, in its pillowcase, all the way home on the 611. The big cod's tail was protruding from the top of the case like a sail and it was still rush hour so there were plenty of people about. Despite that I had the entire row of seats close to the exit to myself, even though the fish were stored in the luggage compartment trolleybuses had beneath the winding stairs. Maybe it had something to do with the fact that I'd had the bag slung over my shoulder and the smell from the bag had clung to my jumper.

The cod, once home, was placed on my dad's garden scales and weighed in at 20 pounds 8 ounces, still my largest cod to this day, challenged only by a fish taken more than 30 years later from a wreck offshore Rye in East Sussex, (another journey that began 'down the Old Kent Road'!) but that was a full 2 pounds under. When we gutted the fish, intact in its stomach was a dab, 11 inches long. I guess that was the small, initial bite I'd felt and the little flattie was then grabbed and swallowed, Jonah-like, whole by the cod.

Another of Teddy's favourites was Deal. Here the boats were launched from the beach, being slid down on a trail of old railway sleepers until they reached the water. Once semi-afloat, it was a case of scrambling over the side, starting the motor, again with the old crank-handle, and motoring a few hundred yards offshore.

Once Brian had his own car we started going there on our own and having been introduced to the local speciality bait, yellowtail lugworm, we always made sure we ordered ours in advance from Tony's Bait Bar, run from his kitchen door, or so it seemed, by one of the biggest names in south coast sea angling of the day, Tony Libby. Our preferred boats were run by Ben Bailey; £3 for the day.

As we left the beach on one trip the skipper told us they'd found a mussel bed not far offshore that was loaded with big plaice, with fish to 5 pounds being captured and that's where we would be fishing. He said there was also the outside chance of a turbot, a larger, more aggressive species than plaice, but similarly flat.

We certainly caught plaice, including some very decent fish bigger than 3 pounds, but then I felt something very different. Plaice are pretty good fighters but this was much more feisty and felt a lot heavier too. I was still using my homemade rod and heavy reel loaded with 30 pound line but there was no winching this straight up. I told Brian and the skipper it was a turbot, for sure, and called across to another couple of boats fishing close by telling them what I was fighting.

Eventually I managed to draw the fish towards the boat, where the skipper waited with a big landing net. He dipped the net over the side and came up with… not a turbot, but a major-league plaice on one hook and the largest mackerel I've ever seen on the other. The plaice weighed 4 pounds 14 ounces and the mackerel, 1 pound 14 ounces when I got them home. Despite the magnificence of the brace, I was ribbed rotten all day, not only by my own boat-mates but every other boat out there.

Probably the most exciting part of the trips to Deal was returning to the beach. The boat had to be steered in to land on the sleepers, while someone on land had a rope to throw aboard, which was tied to a cleat on the bow.

The other end was fixed to a big winch, usually manual with a couple of handles either side, or there were one or two diesel winches and the boat wound up the beach. That was if the sea was calm. If a wind had sprung up during the day, the boat would often be turned sideways by a wave and it was a case of leaping off into as shallow water as possible and wading off: not much fun in March.

Although I was never there when it happened, there were stories of boat turning turtle so it was a bit of a scary event. It makes today's marina-based trips seem soft by comparison – but I'll settle for that every time.

Keith Arthur

The Royalty

The Royalty Fishery, on the Hampshire Avon (most of which isn't in Hampshire, ironically, it's in Wiltshire but so is some of the Bristol Avon – confused?) is a stretch of river with iconic status. Mr Crabtree took Peter there in his delightful book and caught a huge chub: not only a specimen (over 4 pounds) but a monster at 6 pounds 2 ounces. It wasn't worth going to catch that one, as well as being a fictional creature, Mr Crabtree took it home to be set up in a glass case!

The Royalty is in Christchurch, Dorset, close to Mudeford Harbour where the river converges with the Dorset Stour (no other Stours in Dorset, but Essex and Staffordshire have them, as does Kent) and thence to the sea. The Avon is tidal at this point, right up to the famous weirs where every swim has a name. Although some of the swims are named after the famous anglers that have trod the well-kept paths down the years, many are salmon holding spots because the main sport on the river until the coarse season began on June 16th was, and is, salmon fishing which, along with good numbers of sea trout, ran through the stretch on their way to the spawning grounds upstream.

Brian and I had read reports in *Angling Times* of big catches of barbel and chub, mostly caught trotting with big floats from a centrepin reel. One of the experts in the field, F W K Wallis, who was responsible for some magnificent captures on Avon and even held one of the three joint barbel records, made casting from a centrepin so popular, indeed it is said that anglers went to watch him to learn to cast, that the style was named after him. The Wallis Cast involves great timing and top-quality tackle. Having the correct rod helps too, and Brian had a Wallis Wizard, designed for the casting style. Eleven feet long, with a Tonkin cane butt section and split cane top and middle, the rod's slow action helped propel the necessarily heavy floats right across the river, if required, and that same action helped subdue the powerful lunges of strong fish in a heavy current, of which the Avon had, and has, an abundance.

So, when Brian suggested we spend, not a day, but a week on The Royalty, I could hardly refuse. He did the research and booked us in to a small guest house, run exclusively for anglers, in Avon Buildings, a small cul de sac that ends at the main gate to the fishery. Talk about perfect! At the other end of the street, on the corner of Bargates, the main road, is the fishing tackle shop that sold permits, tackle and bait. It is still there today; offering an even better service than it did then, especially in the bait department. Mind you, that is only because angling styles and bait requirements have changed. Brian and I took our Thames tactics, aimed at catching mostly dace on our more local river but with which we caught a few barbel each year, and the occasional chub. That involved using a bait dropper to introduce a lot of maggots at the start then regular additions, via the dropper, through the day. We both ordered a gallon of maggots each day and Davis Tackle, the shop on the corner, wasn't used to that kind of bait requirement then; most of the anglers who fished the river used cheese or sausagemeat for barbel, or lobworms and bread for chub. Nowadays I doubt that an order like that would faze them one bit – indeed I fished there, for the first time in decades, recently and it is a truly magnificent tackle (and bait!) emporium.

What we did to guarantee our maggots was to have them delivered by train to Christchurch Station, just a couple of hundred yards up the road: the Railway Bridge is one of the most famous Royalty swims! The maggots arrived fresh from the Yorkshire bait farm each day, in the old-fashioned square biscuit tins – Middlemass Biscuits was the usual logo on the tins yet I never saw any of their biscuits on the shelves of my local Co-op, where I'd accompanied my mother on many occasions. Maybe they were the 'loose' biscuits that were sold by weight, (anyone else remember that?) with string through two holes for carrying and sacking over the top of the tins. I bet the old train guard was careful they didn't tip over! I am not exactly sure, but I seem to recall 10/6d (52p) a gallon, delivered, as the price. Don Baits was certainly the company!

This was 1966, the year England's football team carried the Jules Rimet Trophy in triumph following the famous World Cup victory and our holiday was for the first week of the tournament. We were both Arsenal fans, North Bank Boys to be precise but with only George Eastham from our club in the squad – and unlikely to play – we didn't mind missing the first couple of games. Checking in to our digs on Saturday morning we strolled the few yards to the gate, more to take in the atmosphere of this, almost sacred, place. The river looked surprisingly small, considering its fame and the bailiff's house stood guard proudly over it. Ken Keynes was the bailiff and we introduced ourselves, saying we would be there every day for the week to come. He told us some of the more important rules (mostly no taking trout, sea trout or salmon!) and we stood for a long while, watching the water swirl and eddy under the footbridge before hurtling round the bend down to The Rapids. It looked awesome! When the Thames ran this fast it was like supersonic cocoa, but this river was crystal clear: fronds of *ranunculus* waving in the current, belying the depth.

Keith Arthur

The gates to the fishery didn't open until 7am, so next morning we were up by 6am, eating our egg and bacon and collecting our flask and packed lunch, our maggots having been collected the night before for the first two days: no Sunday deliveries.

We were waiting outside, not alone either, as Mr Keynes swung the gate open and we decided to walk downstream, to the less popular area towards the bypass bridge where the A35 crosses the river on its way to, or from, Bournemouth. We had decided to fish the Telegraph Pole swim where the river ran fairly deep on the nearside, shallowing up to big banks of *ranunculus* just beyond mid-river, then gravel shallow sloping gently to grass bank.

One of the more intriguing features of The Royalty is that whilst the Avon flows through some of the most beautiful, verdant countryside the south of England has to offer and the area around the coast can be spectacular, the surroundings on this section are quite austere. The land is flat water meadow, with the odd hedge here and there, clumps of dock and nettle with The Pipes, where two large, green pipes cross the river; the Railway Bridge, where several large green (in those days) trains cross the river and the Bypass Bridge where thousands of cars, vans and lorries cross the river. Peaceful it isn't!

I was hoping to catch my big fish on a 12 foot, tubular steel Taperflash rod or a 14 foot fibreglass Float King, bought to match my Float Queen reel, which, in reality, was a rebadged J W Young's centrepin. Brian had his Allcock's Match Aerial, the king of centrepin reels. We had read many times about Dick Walker's special 'fluted floats', carved from balsa wood with a deep groove in each of the four sides. The idea was that these floats gripped the flow, keeping the bait travelling downstream in a straight line. Walker had

Fishing

commented that bait dragged across the current was unlikely to be taken and my experiences since have confirmed just that: dragging bait is the kiss of death! Our floats carried a good amount of shot, 5AAA - 3SSG, which made a much bigger impact on my rod when winding in than on Brian's, which was, of course, purpose built for such a job.

The first day went quite badly: apart from a few roach and dace, plus a chub for Brian, we caught very little until lunchtime. The main problem was the wind, which was blowing across the barren landscape opposite, making our float drag in towards the bank. Even with all that shot, every time we tried to slow the tackle down to make our bait behave as naturally as we could (the water at the bottom of a river is slower than at the surface, because of friction), the wind simply picked up the line and pushed the floats towards the stone-clad bank. So, sandwiches in hand, we deserted our tackle and walked back to the bridge by the bailiff's house, crossed the river and went to the far side to see if wading was possible.

When we arrived we found that not only was it possible but perfect! The gravel shallows were rock-hard underfoot – and populated with what seemed like several million minnows – and the fringe of *ranunculus* would keep us screened from the fishes' view. Having collected our fairly meagre stack of tackle, and our dwindling stock, maggots of course, we set up base camp directly opposite our starting position. As long as no one came and sat where we had previously, everything would be tickity-boo.

It was slightly more difficult to use our bait droppers but by adopting a gentle underarm lob with our rods we managed it and during the afternoon our success rate flourished. As one of us hooked a decent fish, the other would lay his rod on pre-placed rod rests, where we had placed our landing net, and wade downstream to intercept the hooked fish before it made the sanctuary of the weedbeds. It was here that I learned something about the behaviour of chub, in particular, that has stayed with me ever since.

Brian had hooked a decent chub, maybe 3 pounds, and it had set off downstream, causing him to yield it some line to prevent a breakage. I collected the net and set off in pursuit. About 20 yards down I could see Brian's float jagging away and, 6 feet below that, the chub causing the jags. It was twisting and turning in the current until, for some reason I couldn't fathom, it suddenly swam forward, towards Brian. He maintained tension on the line by winding in but the fish was able to swim to its left and into the waving fronds of *ranunculus*, where it simply opened its mouth, grabbed a gobful of weed, shook its bullet-shaped head and swam away. The hook was transferred into the weed and, if I hadn't seen it myself, I would never have believed it. I can't even begin to estimate how many times that has happened to me, and other anglers I have fished with since then, the latest occasion was on the River Colne in Uxbridge last season. It is a trick that I believe is unique to chub and obviously an instinct. One thing is for sure: it is damnably effective!

Following a successful day we decided to try the local fleshpots to see what was on offer. After a decent enough fish and chip 'tea', it was time for drink – and to try our luck. The pubs in Christchurch that we tried were all what I'd call 'drinkers': places where people, mostly blokes with the occasional wife in tow, go to stand and drink. Not much opportunity to find some female company. We considered that by heading towards Mudeford we might happen across some jovial holidaymakers, hopefully with nubile, young daughters who would be grateful to be whisked away for a port and lemon and a touch of passion. Not a prayer! We caught a bus to Mudeford and had a good look around, by which time it was 9.30pm and we scarcely saw a soul, certainly not any escapees from whatever holiday camps were close by – if any.

The return journey was even more desolate. The buses, and it appeared everything else, had stopped operating and the long trudge along the dark main road was a long one. The latest Hammer Horror movie, starring Vincent Price of course, was *The Gorgon*, the 'monster' being a female with snakes in her hair. Brian said: "It's as if The Gorgon was about. There's not one single person alive." It was precisely like that; 10pm and no lights, no cars, no people. The Gorgon became our standing joke: every time we went into a place that was, shall we say, lacking atmosphere, one of us would ask if The Gorgon had been. The usual response was: "Don't know any Gordon mate, sorry."

We had some decent catches that week, mostly chub and barbel that, although not plentiful, came at reasonable enough regularity to make every cast potentially fruitful. It was quite hard work, standing up to our thighs in water and continuously striving to keep the line taut to the float, enabling us to strike at any bite that may happen, so on the Thursday I decided to have a change. I had asked Mr Keynes about the dace and he suggested fishing the point opposite the house where the river turned 90° towards the rapids; the bend forming a smashing 'crease', caused by the point of the bend generating a slack area where the flow came back on itself, leaving a series of swirls denoting a change of depth and current. I used the longer rod in this swim and a much lighter float: one of my trusty Thames crow quills, as the water was no more than 3 feet deep. By the end of the day I had caught one of the best dace bags I am ever likely to see: 108 of them and a single roach. Keepnets were allowed so I was able to count them back into the river as I returned them. I measured every fish and only counted the 'goers', fish over the minimum size limit that, in the case of Royalty dace, was 9 inches. A 9-inch dace will weigh 6 ounces on average so considering that was the minimum size, and I must have landed close to 60 pounds of dace, an amazing bag of fish.

I still have the picture of my best bag from the Telegraph Pole: six chub and three barbel, with a best chub weighing possibly 3 pounds and a barbel that might scrape 5 pounds. We didn't weigh any of the fish because there were special, almost ceremonial scales at the bailiff's house – in the lodge – where specimens could be weighed and the one we most wanted was a 10 pound barbel. Neither of us came close to achieving it – on that trip anyway.

On the last day Brian suggested we try for a sea trout, which we could, basically steal and take home. Our coarse fishing day ticket was 10 bob (50p) but a sea trout ticket was more money, although no rod licence was required because The Royalty was managed by the water company that issued rod licences and a percentage of the day ticket was attributed to the licence fee, a great idea considering how many holidaymakers were attracted to this Mecca of river fishing. *The* sea trout swim was under the bypass bridge, where the fish sheltered out of the flow taking a breather on their upstream journey from the sea. We had to be careful, because legend had it that Mr Keynes spent his days peering through binoculars, watching out for exactly the sort of thing we were doing. It didn't take long to catch one; I was soon attached to a mad, jumping thing that seemed determined to make the carriageway above. We eventually netted it, gave it a quick bash on the noggin with a large piece of gravel and slid it lengthwise into my rod holdall. All we had to do was walk to the lodgings, collect our small suitcases – clothes were far less abundant then; a couple of shirts and a change of underwear was about it – and make our way to the train station.

Keith Arthur

We were on the 'house' bank and, to our absolute horror, Mr Keynes stepped outside the front door to greet us. He asked if we had enjoyed our fishing, knowing that we were going home at the end of the day. Maybe he knew a lot more because we couldn't get away. I laid my flimsy rod holdall on the gravel outside his house, to rest my shoulder, and the blooming thing started flipping about! Either the trout had a harder head than we'd accounted for or I was a rotten shot with the rock. I pushed it down with my foot, trying to keep it still and my face straight. "Seen any salmon or sea trout?" he asked. Thinking that he had definitely seen us, I replied that we had attempted to catch some of the big roach that hole up by the bypass bridge but had to give up because of the huge numbers of sea trout there. I mentioned that I had actually caught one, by complete accident, and returned it instantly. "As long as you do, son, that's what we like." I am convinced, to this very day, that he knew precisely what had happened.

Brian and I paid a few more visits to The Royalty, up until about 1970 when my concentration on open match fishing took hold and pleasure fishing and, indeed, specimen hunting took a back seat. Our most memorable trip culminated in fishing the Telegraph Pole swim again and, at the very last knockings, I hooked a big barbel. It ran downstream towards a small island, then turned and made its way back upstream. I was fishing from the pole bank, with Brian wading opposite and the fish kept going, past both of us, until it came to a position where I had to run after it, landing net in hand. Eventually I played the fish out and netted it, both of us agreeing it was a 'double': over 10 pounds. Keepnets were banned at this time so I filled my canvas bucket with water, stuck the barbel in headfirst and packed up as fast as possible, meeting Brian at the bailiff's house. I dumped my kit outside and as I did so a somehow familiar face peered out of the room, cigar in mouth, teacup in hand. "What've you got there boy?" he asked. The penny dropped: it was none other than the legendary Jack Harrigan, Royalty angler supreme who even had a swim named after him at that time, and it survives to this day. Harrigan's is just downstream of The Pipes, on the far bank to the house.

"I've got a barbel, Mr Harrigan."

He asked how big, so I lifted it from the bucket.

"Might make 11 that one, it's a cracker," he said and my heart leapt!

I carried the fish into the weighing room to the scales, a big chromed pan on a balance, just like in the old-time fishmongers. I, rather ambitiously, placed the 10 pound and 2 pound weights on the balance, with the fish on the pan. The scale never moved. I grudgingly lifted off the 2 pound and the pan rocked but the needle didn't tilt. The fish wasn't quite big enough.

"Never mind boy" he said. "Weight it out anyway." It was close though, with the 8 pound, 1 pound and 8 ounces weight on the balance it was still in the fish's favour but it wouldn't make 9 pounds 12 ounces. Using some of the weights that were really tiny scraps of lead foil, I got it to 9 pounds 10 ounces and change: not quite 8dr but more than 4dr, so I called it 9.10.6. Up until a few short years ago it was still my personal best (pb): in fact it took a trip to the other Avon in Wiltshire, the Bristol one, with my *Tight Lines* colleague Nigel Botherway and a film crew, to beat it. The first barbel I landed that day looked close too and so it was, 9 pounds 13 ounces but the very next fish did the trick: my first double at 10 pounds 3 ounces. Amazingly I have caught three more 'barneys' (barney rubbles = doubles) since then and two of those have been on tape for *Tight Lines* too, as have been my pb tench and bream! If the cameras we use for our films cost a touch less than the £45,000 they do, I might be tempted to slip one in my tackle bag.

Keith Arthur

Blenheim Palace

During the formative years of my fishing, reading the angling weeklies was a must. I absorbed much of what I read, unlike at school where, although I could still conjugate the odd Latin verb – and most of them were very odd – a great deal disappeared over my head with a fairly loud whoosh. For instance, I can still recall many of the old record fish from the British Record Fish List of the time, possibly because, once caught, record fish were usually taken away to be preserved forever by the taxidermist's art. Nowadays they are returned alive from whence they came and the same fish are targeted by anglers that want to catch a record without, necessarily, doing the appropriate legwork and research to find it.

As well as records, there is a certain kudos to catching 'specimen' fish. Each species has an acknowledged specimen size and to achieve that target is considered extremely worthy. By the mid-1960s I may have possibly caught one specimen: that perch on my Maskell's roach pole from the Waverley, depending on whether I could accept my own estimates. In reality, it wasn't weighed so it didn't count.

Some of those specimen sizes would seem very generous today, a 4 pound chub, 6 pound bream, 20 pound carp and 5 pound tench being the most obvious. Match anglers on competitions, never mind dedicated big-fish hunters, catch many fish of those sizes week-in, week-out. It's not general though as a 2 pound roach, 1 pound dace and 20 pound pike are still *very* big fish; indeed I'd say that it is more difficult to catch a 2 pound roach from a river today than it was in 1966.

All that considered, Brian and I fancied a go at a specimen tench and the place just had to be Blenheim Palace. This is the family home of the Duke of Marlborough and was the birthplace of Sir Winston Churchill. The lake, a traditional 'estate lake' designed in the 1760s by Capability Brown, as were so many others, was formed by damming the River Glynne and cutting the contours of the lake from the surrounding gardens, which had already been created by John Vanbrugh. The bridge that spans the lake was designed to traverse three streams, created by Vanbrugh from the Glynne, and when Brown flooded the lake, part of the visible bridge structure was hidden which, in many experts' opinions, actually improved the view.

We'd thought that Blenheim was 'at Oxford', reached from London by a journey along the A40 which, back then, was a long way from the trunk road that it became and even further from the M40 which came to pass many years later. The problem was that Brian hadn't had his car (the Lotus Cortina!) long so we didn't know how long the journey would take. We'd also learned that Blenheim wasn't actually *at* Oxford (the city) but *in* Oxford (the county) and wasn't even on the A40. Bearing those facts in mind, we decided on an early start, to leave Brian's parents' pub (The Old Crown on Highgate Hill, remember?) at 3am. This wasn't an unknown time to leave for a day's fishing, in fact I travelled as a guest on a North London Angling Club coach trip with Brian, the club being based at the pub, and the first pick-up, at Archway Station, was at 2am. That was scheduled to get us to Ringwood, on the Hampshire Avon, for a 6am start and, as Ringwood looked about as far as Woodstock (where Blenheim stands) we thought that as we had no other pick-ups, a 3am start should allow us to arrive at Blenheim just before the gates opened to anglers at 6am. What we hadn't considered was that Brian drove everywhere at 100mph, at least, (there were no 70mph limits on major roads) while the North London charabanc probably had a top speed closer to 50mph. So it was shortly before 4.30am when we pulled up at the gates.

Tench fishing is now, in these days of no close season, at its best from late-April to late-June, in my and many others' opinions, so the most likely chance of success at catching a specimen tinca (the Latin name for tench is *tinca tinca* and I didn't learn that from *The Latin Way* with Mr Hutchings at school), would be as close to the start of the season, June 16th, as possible. The 'first day' fell on a Friday and that was fully booked when Brian applied, well before the old season closed, in March, but he managed to get us fixed up for the Monday, June 19th; a fantastic opportunity, as there was no fishing at Blenheim on Sundays. We felt that the tench would have a chance to find out what bait was on the Friday and Saturday then, having had the luxury withdrawn on Sunday, they'd be gagging for it on Monday, especially as no one would have fished for them at all since the previous October.

Never being one to skimp on anything, Brian had made sure we wouldn't run out of bait and as it was the first full week of the season, we'd both booked a week off work that, for me, was selling furniture and for Brian, was training to be a chef at the Café Royal in London's West End. Any bait left over could be used up easily during that week. Our load was six uncut loaves, half a sack of brown breadcrumb groundbait, ready-mixed with water for instant introduction to the lake, and two gallons of maggots. Groundbait was banned but silly things like bans didn't stop Brian – or me for that matter – and as long as we could get it on to the boat, it would be deposited into the lake as soon as we found our chosen spot.

Keith Arthur

Fishing at Blenheim is from punts only and the estate has 16 of them, designed for angling, in a boathouse on the lake. Boat keys are allocated by the estate manager at the gatehouse, once booking details are verified, then it's a bit of a Le Mans start and a sprint through the estate to park at the boathouse, relocate the gear from the car boot into the punt then a Steve Redgrave-type row across the lake to the chosen swim. As we were first there – well, we were 90 minutes early – we felt we were in pole position and felt that a quick nap was in order, to refresh us after the white-knuckle ride through the West London suburbs and Buckinghamshire and Oxfordshire countryside.

We woke up to the sound of crunching gravel and screeching metal as the gate was swung open and anglers, who had been standing, as against sleeping, outside, queued at the gatehouse. I stumbled out, bleary-eyed, and was handed a key, about sixth or seventh in line. Brian had the Lotus engine running and I dived into the passenger seat but because the final part of our trip was along pathways inside the estate, the car's power was negated due to the fact overtaking was totally impossible: we'd been caught, quite literally, napping! Possibly even more daunting was the fact that our key was for boat number 13.

On parking up, we did the unload and reload but when it came to unlocking the padlock securing the punt, it was an entirely different matter. The mooring chain, which doubled as an anchor chain, had been twisted and tangled and by the time we'd finished trying to release the lock, every other boat was out of the boathouse and paddling across the lake.

Brian had done some more homework on the best spots and he'd been drawn a map of the lake by a customer of the pub who had fished it many times. *The* spot was a big bay on the far side of the lake at an angle of about

30° from the moorings. Every boat was headed in that direction so we thought we might as well not bother with that; after all we appeared to have the rest of the lake completely to ourselves, with the exception of a single punt that was being rowed to the left-hand end of the lake.

Almost directly opposite the boathouse a huge willow cast a massive shadow on the lake, with a big reedbed running away from it to the right as we looked. A decision was made to row over towards the willow, deposit our illicit cargo of groundbait some way short of the reeds then drift into the bank, anchor up and fish over our baited patch. For a day that started so dramatically badly, it didn't take long for things to improve markedly, as the plan worked a treat – so far as rowing, dumping and anchoring went anyway. All we had to do now was to decide tactics.

Great anglers such as Richard Walker and Fred J Taylor had told us through their writings of exploits at Wootten Lake that the best way to fish for tench was by using 'the lift method', where split shot sufficient to sink the float easily were employed between 6 and 8 inches from the hook, with the depth of the float adjusted so it lay flat on top of the water, the entire weight of shot lying on the bottom. Once in place, the line was tightened to 'cock' the float. Any fish taking the baited hook would move the shot, causing the float to either disappear from sight or assume the lying flat on the water position; lifting, as the method described.

We both set up lift method rigs, using unpainted lengths of peacock quill as floats, attached to the line by a single rubber sleeve at one end. I had my trusty Taperflash match rod and centrepin reel, Brian had a beautiful split cane 'Avocet' rod, designed for specimen fishing, and a Rapidex centrepin. Brian suggested that I should start with maggots as bait, whilst he'd use breadflake; the white crumb, torn from the centre of the loaf and lightly wrapped around the shank of the hook and pinched at the top, around the point where the line was tied to the hook. We both had 4 pound breaking strain line and size 10 hooks, which is what Walker and Taylor both advised.

We simultaneously swung our baited rigs over the furtively-groundbaited area, my hook adorned by five wriggling maggots, Brian's with a fluffy white pinch of bread. Two minutes later and Brian's rod was bent in half as he was into his first tench. It looked like a '5' and was placed, with some ceremony, into his keepnet. I was still biteless.

A few minutes later the scene was repeated with a similar-sized tench joining his mate in Brian's net. Three further fish down the line and I was beginning to think that, just maybe, this was to be a bread day and removed my maggots. As I did so Brian netted a super roach, at least 1 pound, and confined it to his waiting keepnet to join his red-eyed, green mates. As soon as my bread touched down, the float settled, lifted then shot away and I was fighting my first Blenheim tench and, possibly, my first specimen fish.

The morning continued in much the same vein, with fish after fish falling to our breadflake: the groundbait, illegal as it was, had done a pretty good job and I couldn't imagine that there was any left on the bottom, the way that shrouds of bubbles had been rising from the lake bed as fish after fish tore into the silty, weedy bottom trying to garner some nourishment from what amounted to no more than bread dust.

Around 1pm we stopped for a lunch break, usually something well worth doing when angling alongside a trainee chef, especially from the Café Royal: the sandwiches were always first class. The early start and exertions of the drive, followed by a very long morning catching fish had slightly got the better of us so we settled down for a brief shuteye period before resuming the assault on the tench gathered for the feast in front of us. I don't know if it was then that Brian told me the Café Royal 'Blue Trout' story. It may well not have been but this seems as good a point as any to relate it.

One of the restaurant's most famous signature dishes was the aforementioned 'Blue Trout'. The recipe calls for a live trout to be stunned, the guts are removed via a small hole cut in the intestine and the fish is then soaked in vinegar, briefly, until it assumes a blueish hue. Once this is achieved the trout is transferred to a tureen containing *court bouillon*, a herby, thin vegetable soup being a reasonable description. The tureens at the Café Royal were, according to Brian, huge copper things with ornamental lids and handles and as the fish cooked very quickly, no more than six to eight minutes, the cooking procedure took place as the tureen made the journey from kitchen to dining room in the 'dumb waiter'.

Being a classic and very high-class establishment, the waiters are highly trained, especially in the serving of food, therefore when the tureen arrived at the guest's table the waiter would take up his serving implements: fork and spoon held between index finger, second finger, and thumb, lift the lid and reach into the tureen to catch the now-cooked trout. It was a sign of poor training if the waiter looked for the fish: everything was done by feel.

One of Brian's tasks was to prepare the trout as a more senior chef prepared the stock and tureen, with Brian, as junior, then popping the trout in. One day a waiter gave Brian a hard time, complaining that the trout he had been given to serve was not 100% fresh, so, by way of response, Brian sent down a troutless blue trout tureen, then stood outside the glass door watching as the unfortunate waiter fished around interminably for something that wasn't there. Eventually he had to look and, finding no more than the *bouquet garni*, replaced the tureen on the trolley with far less flourish than which it was removed and sent it back, via the dumb waiter to the kitchen, whereupon congratulations were handed round. The senior chef had so much fun he repeated the trick a second time, having told the waiter that the first trout was so fresh it must have jumped out in the lift. After the second empty pot, the waiter got the message.

Awakening from our well-earned rest we were quite surprised to see most of the anglers who had rowed across to the bay were now searching for swims in the part of the lake we were now smugly sat in, both with bulging keepnets. Brian, always one to wind other anglers up, suggested that we were hardly likely to improve on our respective catches, so it might be a good time to pull up our nets, weigh the fish and show the faster starters what they'd rowed past. We didn't do it quietly either, with much: "… I think mine's snagged on the bottom, it's so heavy," and "How many did you say you caught?" The actual numbers are tattooed on my brain: my net contained 19 tench, Brian had 21 and that roach. I was to weigh first, so I picked out what appeared to be the biggest and placed it in the canvas bucket that had once contained 20 pounds of breadcrumb that we'd thrown into the lake. Brian called it at "4 pounds 14 ounces." His first fish weighed exactly the same and, between us, we had 11 at that weight and not a single fish reached the magic 5 pounds. Brian's solitary roach tipped the scales to 1 pound 4 ounces so we had experienced one hell of a great day's fishing and would be home, or at least back at The Old Crown, early enough to tell the tale many times over the evening.

For some inexplicable reason I never returned to Blenheim to fish, although I was there a few years ago working at the CLA Game Fair. It is a truly magnificent place and as I watched a group of angling coaches giving free instruction to youngsters and new anglers on the lake above the top bridge, where the River Glynne first starts to widen out, I thought back the

30-odd years to that day and those wonderful tench.

Only bream and roach, both of which now provide the bulk of anglers' summer catches, with some big pike and perch during the colder months, were caught by the angling novices and their tutors but some of those bream were 5 pounds and more. Not specimens, then or back in the 1960s, but superb fish caught in what are among the most beautiful surroundings in which I have ever fished. I've caught a few 5 pound tench since then, plus a few 'sixes', up to nearly 7 pounds. In fact 6 pounds 14 ounces is my current personal best and do you know I reckon a specimen is probably 7 pounds these days, so I'm still a measly 2 ounces light. But not a whole blue trout.

The Kentish Stour

Never Pick Tomatoes…

Sturry was one of the great destinations on the Kentish Stour. It was where the clear water section of the river that flowed through Canterbury, famed for its trout, roach and dace, changed to a more coloured section, where roach and bream became the target. The reason was the sewage works.

A couple of hundred yards downstream from the road bridge a pipe poured treated effluent into the Stour. Nowadays 'treated effluent' looks more like purified water but back then it wasn't. 'Treatment' entailed taking the material from our bathroom activities, spreading it out into what looked like roundabouts for seagulls – they could always be seen standing on the spray-bars that rotated above the spread-out… well, you get the picture, and spraying water on it to separate the solids from the remainder. The water resulting from the spraying washed through the pipe into the river.

Once the sewage had been 'treated' it was spread over the fields and, being more or less pure fertiliser, everything grew in massive abundance. The nettles were enormous, the grass grew like wheat and the whole area was a sea of green leaves and, occasionally, yellow blossom.

We normally fished Sturry in winter as the extra colour and, it seemed, warmth, entering the river kept the fish feeding when, above the pipe, things ground to a halt. Trotting down with breadflake, using a fairly big cork bodied crow quill float taking 4 or 5 BB shot, 3 pound line and a size 10 hook, would produce roach averaging 10 ounces, with pretty frequent 1 pound+ specimens but once the bream muscled in it would be two-pounder following two-pounder. Groundbaiting wasn't that important, just the occasional handful of mashed bread would keep the shoals searching for more. Unlike many other rivers, maggots were just about a waste of time and money. Using them produced less, and far smaller, fish.

Once arriving at the river the decision was whether to sit above the stink-pipe and fish for dace, or walk that bit further and try for, usually with some success, a bag of bream. I was usually quite 'worthy' and would sit on the clear section of river, watching beds of *ranunculus* swaying in the flow, catching a few dace up to 8 ounces; a decent average size – for dace. Bread was a waste of time for them, maggots were essential, but those dace were beautiful fish, especially nearing the end of the season when the males would develop extremely rough skin and an almost golden tinge to their flanks. Their pectoral and anal fins would take on a coral-coloured hue, the females bearing a pewter shade, plump bellies a give-away of the next intention.

The roach caught above the pipe were blue of back, scarlet of fin and orange-eyed, often bearing evidence of 'blackspot' a parasite that affects fish in clear water. Stour roach were not the long fish of the Thames shape I was used to, but dumpy, big-shouldered fish that thumped the rod end when hooked. These too would feast on maggots but bites were harder to get than below the pipe; often in really cold conditions half a dozen fish in a day was the most that could be reasonably expected. Below the pipe, almost regardless of temperature, fish would feed well.

My most frequent companion to Sturry was Big John. John ran a West Indian fruit and vegetable stall in Ridley Road market in Dalston. Ridley Road was once a famous Jewish market, where the British fascist Sir Oswald Mosley famously met with his 'Black Shirts', berating the immigration policies that allowed Jewish immigrants refuge from European persecution.

By the mid-1960s the Caribbean culture was well established in the East End, the Jewish former residents having moved out to Stanmore and Edgware as their businesses thrived. John sold his yams, plantains and mangoes to a regular and flourishing clientele. He earned the nickname 'Big John' long before the song of that name became popular, mostly because he was BIG! Weighing 24 stone plus, he was an awesome sight sitting on his fishing basket, bringing a whole new meaning to the term hangover. There was certainly potential for parking a bike!

John had been an excellent sportsman, gaining the excess timber when his swimming and football days came to a close following a leg injury. Once on, it stayed on, at least for many years. In 1989 I saw Big John for the first time in 15 years and he was a shadow of his former self, although still 'well-made', probably nudging 15 stone or so. I asked for the secret of his weight loss, maybe a mistake as it was stress-related, induced by his wife Carole leaving him and the ensuing messy (aren't they always?) divorce.

When we fished together though, John was always the life and soul of the party, with an infectious laugh that was never more evident than when he told a joke – and he was full of jokes! Often his laugh created more mirth than the punchline and when John was driving we'd often have to pull over until the tears left his eyes.

By far the most memorable trip to Sturry involved Carole too and was taken at the start, rather than the end, of the fishing season, during a glorious, warm July day.

We left their Dalston home in John's pride and joy, a luxurious Austin

Westminster car. This was the limousine of its day, with leather seats that smelt of class and a burr walnut fascia and door panels. It even had carpet and a radio, by no means standard features in the 1960s, AND an automatic gearbox.

Fishing tackle seemed to fit in car boots then too, especially a boot as capacious as the Westminster's so, loaded with tackle, Carole, picnic, complete with tartan picnic blanket and associated impediments, essential with women on board, we set off for Canterbury.

It was a magnificent day and the river looked perfect, albeit too weedy for my liking above the pipe. Downstream however, the extra turbidity created by the outflow from the sewage farm prevented weed growing and the river ran swiftly but smoothly.

Big John set up close to the pipe in an area with a brick wall maybe 7 or 8 yards behind him: plenty wide enough for the blanket to be spread and Carole to sit in comfort. I sat myself 25 yards further downstream, at the beginning of a bend, with slacker water on the inside, allowing me to 'lay-on' by adding extra split shot that would sink the float under normal circumstances but, with the weight lying on the bottom, affording me reasonably delicate presentation of a still bait on the bottom.

Bread was the obvious bait, even in summer, as the coloured water held a mass of bootlace eels, never more than a foot or so long, and as slimy as could be imagined. They also swallowed the hook every time and catching one meant not only nets and hands (and trousers where the hands were wiped) covered in slime but also the trouble of tying on a new hook. Eels don't like bread.

John preferred to trot his bait down so was happy using maggots; eels rarely chase after moving bait. He also intended to catch roach, my quarry were bream, and loads of them so I'd have nets, hands and trousers equally, or even more, slimier than if I'd suffered the plague of bootlaces, but a 2 pound bream every cast beats the hell out of a mini-snake each drop.

It wasn't long before John was catching good roach, which meant Carole had to have a go; she was becoming bored just watching. Trotting a river with reasonable flow isn't an easy task for the inexperienced so John set her a rod up to fish on the bottom, similar to how I was fishing.

Of course, maggots were John's bait so Carole was suffering the eel plague I'd avoided. This was not pleasing John one bit as, instead of hooking and landing quality roach, as he had been, he was having to grasp 10 to 12 inches of wriggling, slimy eel, search for the hook and when it couldn't be seen, cut the line, releasing the eel back to its watery home.

Eventually he cracked and told Carole she'd have to stop fishing and set up the picnic. Out came the sandwiches, lovely little paper plates and doilies – completely foreign to our usual bankside fare which was more likely to be a pork pie in John's case, or a packet of cakes in mine.

It was then that Carole discovered she'd forgotten the tomatoes but, as luck would have it, there were some growing in the field behind. She climbed up on to the brick wall separating field from riverbank and started to walk towards the flourishing crop of bright red fruits, freely growing on their vines, seemingly wild as there were no fences or any sign of restriction from reaching them.

John, noticing Carole's absence, turned just in time to see her step off the wall onto the field, towards her goal. "STOP!" he shouted, almost screaming, loud enough for me to turn in shock to see what was going on.

"DON'T WALK ON THAT!" John continued. "Don't worry," Carole said. "There are no fences; it's not private."

Keith Arthur

One step later it became clear that John's warning hadn't come in time, Carole sinking to just below her armpits, prevented only by her voluminous chest, from disappearing completely into the damp, soft ground. John was sitting in front of where the sewage was spread from the settlement beds and, as tomato seeds aren't digestible, where the plants were growing in abundance.

Once the crust covering the ground was broken the composition of what lay beneath was patently obvious: it didn't half stink!

The next problem was removing Carole, plugged into the ground like it was quicksand. She might have been a pretty big girl, but she was sylph-like compared to John, and even I was no lightweight.

We spread as much of the luxuriant foliage as we could on the ground between the wall and Carole and then inched our way towards her. Between us we managed to draw her free, accompanied by sucking sounds from the soft ground and waves of unbelievably noxious pong.

Once out it was plain that she couldn't remain covered in – well, what she was covered in, so she had to strip down to her 'smalls', although that may not be a fully accurate description, and wash herself and outer garments in the river; in the clear water upstream of the pipe.

Luckily she had the picnic blanket to wrap herself in and the sun to dry her clothes and, of course, we had to wait until everything was dry before we could go home, so we might as well get on with the fishing.

To be absolutely honest I can't remember how the day ended, as far as what we caught is concerned, but I will never forget the sight of Carole's head and shoulders sticking out of the swamp, nor the smell that followed.

I don't know how many times John told that tale in the ensuing years but it was one of those that entailed stopping the car – or van – to wipe away the

The best excuse for loafing in the countryside

tears of laughter.

Laughter wasn't the only reason for John to stop either. One of the other destinations on the Kentish Stour that became a winter Mecca for anglers was Plucks Gutter. Huge shoals of roach would be forced upstream from the estuary at Sandwich Bay by increasing salt tides during dry winter weather, only to meet more of the same being forced downstream by water cleared by regular frosts. Grove Ferry and the slightly deeper Plucks Gutter were the places to be.

Or usual tackle requirements would only be a couple of rods, landing net handle and a few banksticks, to take keepnet and rod rest heads. That lot was in one rod holdall, and our wicker – or for those who wanted the best, jungle cane – baskets were filled with the rest of the essential impedimenta such as reels, float boxes and so on, plus bait; three or four pints of maggots. Eight of us easily fitted into Big John's Commer van.

Alongside and amongst us would be the residue of John's Saturday trading; the odd box of plantain and hessian sacks containing yam and the like. The smell, even before we boarded, could best be described as interesting.

This vehicle was very much John's workhorse, used for collecting his wares from the original Covent Garden, which meant there were no seats in the back. We simply lined our baskets up either side to sit on and stacked the fruit and vegetable cases and sacks in the centre, using them as footrests.

There is one day that sticks longest in my mind, even thought the fishing itself was not much to write home about. We had left Dalston at 6.30am – via the Dunkirk Café of course – but with a high tide due at around dusk, 4.30pm, we decided to wait for that. One of the group, Alec – a pensioner who was known to tell the odd porkie when it came to reporting his catch as

Fishing

you will see later – said he'd had a few big roach but mostly it was a case of a few smallish redfins and occasional dace, plus the ubiquitous bootlaces, still a plague, even in winter. With little to show for our persistence, we loaded the kit back into the van, lining our baskets up against the sides so we could at least lean back against the metal panels, using our folded Barbour jackets (the Solway Zipper was *del rigeur* for all match fishermen then, the only jacket known to man that would happily stand up on its own all day, such was the stiffness of the wax-treated material) as bolsters.

John was driving, his equally large fellow Ridley Road stall-holder Mickey would be riding shotgun in the cab, whilst I rode in the back with Billy H and Alec. By the time we departed The Gutter it was pitch black and a long journey lay ahead.

The swaying of the laden van made me a bit sleepy so, despite the lack of a proper seat, I suppose I must have dozed off. I suddenly awoke to find everything dark, cold and, worse of all dead still! I was freezing and thought we had probably crashed. I could tell we were the right way up because my cap was still on my head, so I delved into a pocket to find my lighter – I was a smoker until 1985 – to attempt to find out what had happened.

Bill was fast asleep on the opposite side of the van, Alec had found that a sack of yams made a decent mattress and John and Mickey were both snoring their respective heads off in the front. I looked at my watch and saw it was nearly 10pm, so goodness only knows how long we'd been there – plus I didn't even know where 'there' was!

A few nudges and shakes soon had everyone awake, bar Mickey who could have slept on a tightrope walker's rope. John simply explained that the soporific snoring sounds emanating from the rear and beside him had brought about 'the long blink', so rather than risk dropping off at the wheel, he'd pulled into a lay-by and got his head down: "… for 10 minutes."

We were still quite a distance from the south-eastern suburbs and it was way past closing time when we eventually arrived back in Dalston – and work on Monday morning came.

Keith Arthur

The Kentish Stour II

Mind the Gaps

During the worst of winter, more roach would descend the river from Canterbury and Sturry to Westbere. A friend of Brian's – Percy, a flower-seller, nurseryman (and MUCH more – his smallholding was visited by the police many times searching for the victim of a notorious East End gangland slaying!) owned a little boat, which he kept at Fordwich. The first straight on the river, downstream to an old bailey bridge, was brilliant fishing for roach and bream if the river was carrying a tinge of colour.

If we wanted to fish the top straight, closed to coarse anglers until October as it was the preserve of the fly fishing branch of the Canterbury Angling Club, we'd walk. Percy and Brian were both members of the club but I never joined. I simply sat between them and when the bailiff came round, I'd talk to him as if we were old mates. Not once was I asked for my club membership ticket – just as well too!

We took some phenomenal catches of roach to well over a pound, with bream to double that, in shallow water no more than 3 feet deep. The method was to trot down using a cork-bodied crow quill float taking maybe four or five BB shot and a size 10 hook with a lump of breadflake as bait. Feeding a couple of balls of breadcrumb groundbait at the start, with a small ball every 10-15 minutes, we'd have the fish lined up, even in very cold weather.

Keith Arthur

I recall one day when it was *extremely* cold and Brian had the fish 'lined up' taking one after another by casting almost to the far side. He was using a 12 foot Apollo Taperflash rod, made from tubular steel by the Accles and Pollock Company, that I remember used to, mysteriously, advertise in London Underground trains. The Apollo trademark was certainly a good choice.

The rod was made in three sections, with a series of stepped tapers on the middle section. On one occasion, as Brian cast there was a strange sort of crunching sound and the three piece rod became four piece: it simply snapped on one of the stepped tapers. The only excuse we could think of was the cold making the steel brittle, because I saw another identical breakage on a very cold day.

When the water went clearer we had to move to deeper water, which meant taking a ride in Percy's boat, which boasted a low-powered 'Seagull' outboard motor. More than once the propeller would foul the gravel bed of the river and the shear pin would need to be replaced, as we drifted down with the current. At least we would be heading in the right direction!

Sometimes we would stop a couple of hundred yards below the Bailey bridge, on a double bend, where the flow of the river deepened the water close to the bank. I don't recall catching bream there but when the roach were 'at home', the fishing was astonishing, with fish after fish from ½ pound-1½ pound coming to the net.

When those fish had migrated downstream, it was time for 'The Gaps' at Westbere. These were shallow lakes formed by subsidence generated by the Kentish coal mines which were all over the area, many were long-gone even then but the legacy of Westbere Colliery remained in the form of The Gaps. I suppose the easiest way to describe them would be as smaller versions of the Norfolk Broads. They remained part of the river, separated from the flow for some of their length by huge rush beds, with gaps in between, hence the name.

Those on the left-hand side of the river going downstream were used regularly by wildfowlers as the duck flights in winter were enormous: the sky would darken as the flocks arrived. Prudence got the better of us most of the time and we fished the river alongside.

On the opposite bank of the river, the right-hand side going downstream, was a lake that had been formed similarly, by subsidence, but the bank had been built up to above the highest normal flood level, so the lake was an entity in its own right. We called it Farm Lake and fishing was strictly forbidden, which, as any angler will tell you, made it all the more desirable.

The three of us made some wonderful catches from the river itself down there. The bream were larger and more numerous than at Fordwich and by simply fishing with our float set over-depth and holding the bait still on the bottom – again bread was the best choice – we would have upwards of a dozen bream apiece on a good day, many of them in the 3-4 pound category. There were less roach but they were of a better average stamp. If they didn't feed, then we'd creep over the bank, keeping well down and out of sight, and fish Farm Lake.

The fishing was absolutely unbelievable: truly massive shoals of bream and some magnificent roach were available, and they could be caught very close in, on the bank which ran at right-angles to the river, with a stand of trees hiding us from the farmhouse at the far end of the lake.

Strangely, bread didn't work there: maggots were the answer but not just one or two on a small hook; these fish wanted four or five on a size 10. I can't explain why, but I tried a bunch of maggots on a size 14 hook and caught very little; as soon as I tied on the larger size 10, I caught bream and roach. They must have liked the taste of steel I guess.

Plenty of groundbait was required, 10 large grapefruit-sized balls at the start, followed by a ball after each fish. We had to cast no more than a couple of yards past the end of our rods, any further was a waste of time and effort. We would often catch 30 or 40 bream, from 2½-4 pounds each, in a session but we didn't take liberties and go there each week, we saved it as a treat. I had one extra-special day there, a couple of years later in 1970, but that forms part of another chapter, so I'll tell you about it then.

Ultimately we were rumbled, completely by accident. We were meticulous in covering our tracks: the banks were more or less 'nutty slack', coal chips and small lumps, so any leftover bait stuck out like the sorest of thumbs. We made sure that not a single piece of groundbait would be left, never mind litter, in case someone noticed we'd been fishing there. I could never stand leaving any rubbish behind even then, a habit I have retained although I will often leave some bait for the birds but NOT at Farm Lake.

We were discovered one day when the farmer came down on his tractor to move some logs we'd seen stacked on the riverbank. It was too late to move and make good our escape: it was time to face the music. Percy was closest to the house so, as we heard the tractor, chugging along the bank, he told us that he'd do the talking and to ignore everything, to not even turn round and watch.

The tractor pulled up behind him, with the engine running and the farmer called out: "Oy, you! You're not allowed to fish there." Percy never turned a hair.

"Oy, come on, get-aht-of-it." Still no movement from Perce.

The farmer shut off the engine, plunging it into silence, climbed down from the seat and walked over to where Percy was concentrating on his float.

"Come on mate, pack up; there's no fishing here."

With that, from just a few feet away, Percy jumped as if startled and looked at the farmer, opening and closing his mouth whilst making a sort of grunting sound. By this time Brian and I were turned away, literally holding our sides with laughter.

"Err-err-err-err" offered Percy.

"What did you say?" replied the farmer.

"We're deaf and dumb mate," said Percy, "what do you think I said?"

That did it. Me and Brian were rolling on the ground, beside ourselves with laughter, unlike the farmer who was beside himself with something different. He failed to see the humorous side of the situation and made us pack up.

I never fished The Gaps with Brian and Percy again although several years later Farm Lake was available to anglers on a club ticket, under a different name. Sport wasn't as good because there were more than three people fishing it every so often but the bream were still bigger than average for the area.

At the end of each day's fishing at Fordwich, we'd adjourn to the Fordwich Arms for a meal and a few drinks before driving home. The drink-drive laws of the day were very different, with 'drunk and incapable' being the limit! I was always designated to drive home so I stayed capable, which is far more than can be said for the other two.

As a publican's son, Brian had a fair old capacity, starting with something like a Barley Wine or Stingo, VERY strong ales sold in 'nip' bottles of about a third of a pint. From that he could go to anything in the 'short' department but his usual choice was a port and brandy. Percy would be straight on the 'gold watch' (scotch), in doubles. I'd join him for a couple, keeping my driving duties in mind.

The pub didn't do food on a Sunday evening but Percy's silver tongue persuaded them that when we called in they should cook us each a steak sandwich and after a freezing day on the bank – remember we only went there in the depths of winter – one of those and a couple of scotches went down a treat.

If there was no steak, we'd stop at The Dutch House, a pub on the A20 which we'd take a detour to reach.

I always found the drive home exciting as the two cars Brian owned during this time were far quicker than my own vehicle: a Bedford Dormobile, rigged out with bench seats either side in the back. Brian had a Ford Corsair GT 2000, which he then chopped-in for a Lotus Cortina. Both went like rockets but while the Corsair would get you into orbit round the Earth, by comparison the Cortina would make it all the way to the sun.

This was in the days before the Suez Crisis, which brought us a National Speed Limit: in those days there were NO limits and while 100mph is possible in even relatively modest cars today, it was a very big deal to have a motor that would do 'the ton' then. Brian's cars did the ton regularly, especially when I was taking us home. Percy lived in Bethnal Green and I set myself a target of getting him there in less than an hour.

Keith Arthur

The Birth of the Blockend

In a previous chapter I made fleeting reference to Twiggy, who had the name long before iconic 1960s 'Superwaif' Leslie Hornby took the title. I was always told his real name was Bill Branch, but it may have been Twigg, and he fished for one of the most powerful clubs in London: the Olive Branch. When I first joined the London Anglers Association, Twiggy's eccentric character belied a great angler with what must have been an extremely innovative mind.

At that time legering with a swimfeeder was catching a lot of fish on the Thames and, as we couldn't count any fish in competitions that didn't reach a minimum size limit, finding a way to catch consistently bigger fish was going to lead to success. The standard swimfeeder, a cylinder made from Perspex with lead strip stapled to the side so it could be cast well out and then hold bottom, worked well but it seemed to attract an inordinate amount of undersized fish, mostly because groundbait had to be used to pack either end of the tube to hold a portion of maggots in the middle. With a baited hook hanging a foot or so below, this could be cast out further than anyone could successfully fish with a float and once it had hit the bottom, the breadcrumb groundbait would be forced out by water expanding the crumbs, leaving the maggots to attract fish to the baited hook. It was the groundbait that attracted the small fish. Using it as an attractor when float fishing proved as much, and 5-6-inch roach and dace, well undersized, would plague anyone using it. What

Twiggy did was eliminate the need for groundbait.

Plenty of anglers knew what he did, by that I mean not use groundbait, but no one knew how he achieved it. A few of the people I was fishing with at the time experimented with various things, the most successful being a standard swimfeeder with a piece of Perspex stuck in one end. Maggots could then be poured into the tube and just a single plug of groundbait used to block the other end. It worked but, because there was still 50% of the groundbait being used, it continued to attract too many small fish.

What was needed was to see one of Twiggy's feeders but that was easier said than done. His stock was carried either in his pockets or in the pillowslip he used to transport his maggots. Normal anglers used a canvas rod holdall to carry their rods to the waterside but not Twiggy. His rod and reel was carried already set up, with a big snap-swivel running on the line ready to accept the 'weapon of mass destruction'. We knew that in his other jacket pocket he carried a big box of elastic bands and a box of matches but we didn't know why: he never smoked, for sure. Twiggy used to pop in Brian's pub for a drink but even when plastered could never be pressed into revealing the secrets, except to say it was his blockend. Something needed to be done and Brian found the way.

He invited Twiggy to join us for a trip to Hurley-on-Thames, a lovely stretch of river that we knew he enjoyed, one Boxing Day. Twig, as far as we knew, had no family and loved his fishing. He was an unmistakable figure: I have described his long, flowing mane of curly hair; he also had a fairly pronounced chin and nose, was quite short in stature and round-shouldered. If ever there was a walking Toby jug, it was Twiggy. The other similarity was that he could hold some drink!

I stayed at the pub on Christmas night and on Boxing Day morning we set off to meet Twiggy for the trip. The road was icy; indeed I recall a pretty scary skid as we drove across 'Suicide Bridge' that carries Hornsey Lane across the A1.

The fishing was hard so at lunchtime we adjourned to The Black Boy, a famous pub on the A423 between Maidenhead and Henley, for some lunch (beer), making sure Twiggy had a decent ration while we maintained (a degree of) sobriety. By the 3pm closing time the light was poor enough for us to go home, to The Old Crown, and Twiggy slept most of the way – or maybe passed out – in the back of Brian's car.

An hour or so later we were back at the pub and Brian invited Twiggy in for a 'swift half' before the 5.30pm opening time and while he was in there I slipped out to the car and nicked a blockend from the pillowcase. What I did was, for an angler, open Pandora's Box, releasing a scourge upon fishes. I only needed that brief look and when Twiggy was eventually put into a cab and taken home – both Brian and I had sunk a few by then – I replaced it, amongst the remaining maggots, in his pillowcase but the secret was out, along with an idea of the man's genius.

Legend has it that Twiggy worked as an engineer in plastic moulding and that he built his blockends at work; they were certainly works of art. The main component was a Perspex tube, 2mm thick, much more rigid than simple celluloid, with a base from the same material moulded to the bottom. The sides and base of the tube had slots about 3mm wide and 8mm long, formed in the moulding process. In the centre of the base was a single hole, 2mm wide. A Perspex disc, again with a central hole, that fitted perfectly inside the tube was held in place by the most ingenious method imaginable. An elastic band was threaded through the hole in the base and held in place by half a matchstick. The band was then pulled through the lid and knotted, leaving a loop at the top, again retained in position by the other half of the match. The idea was to pull the loop to remove the lid, fill the tube with maggots then release the band. The pressure of the lid forced the maggots through the slots in the side and base of the feeder, putting them very close to the baited hook. There is the genius! Not only did the removal of the need for groundbait mean less small fish were caught, because the volume of maggots used was increased, more 'bonus' fish such as big perch, roach, chub and even barbel was increased. All we had to do was work out how to make them because, clearly, Twiggy's methods wouldn't be cost effective.

The answer came one evening when I was explaining the mechanics to my pal Billy Allen and the next day I was in Mr Whaley's tackle shop ordering 1,000 empty shot boxes at a penny-farthing (0.5p) each. The shot boxes were small, clear plastic tubs an inch across, with a soft plastic snap-on lid. The next step was a trip to Henry J Nicholls model shop for some sheets of thick celluloid, used for making windows in model aircraft. Billy had a hole punch and a staple gun from his job as a carpet fitter so all we needed now was a good supply of flat lead strip and we knew exactly where to find that! One of my pals, and soon to be team-mates, Billy Harris, was a cable jointer with the London Electricity Board, his job being to repair any cable faults carrying electricity supplies under the streets of East London. The cable was copper, covered in lead sheeting exactly the right thickness for our purposes. When Bill had to replace a damaged section, we got the lead, he kept the copper, illegally of course. Bill promised as much lead as we needed, and more, if we paid him in feeders!

To create the feeders the first job was to cut the celluloid sheet into shape: whatever length we wanted for the feeders, making longer ones to carry more feed, by 4½ inches across. Holes were made using the punch and the celluloid rolled into a tube of an inch diameter which was then secured by stapling the lead strip to its length, allowing half an inch to fold over at each end. A loop of 8 pound breaking strain line was then placed under the top loop of line before applying the final staple. For the base of the feeder we removed the lid and stapled the bottom half of the box over the bottom of the tube and for the top we put the lid on the box then cut, using a Stanley knife, the bottom off, stapling just below the lip of the box to the completed feeder. The lid could be taken off for filling the feeder. All we didn't have was a means of pushing the maggots out, the action performed by Twiggy's elastic band, but experiments proved that, in a decent current, they were washed out of the holes anyway, provided the holes were big enough.

Using them proved a complete revelation and it is difficult to imagine that such a simple invention could change the face of match fishing for such a long time. Even today there are few methods as effective for fishing medium to large rivers as the blockend. It stayed very much on the Thames for many years, as did much swimfeeder fishing, primarily because using swimfeeders was not allowed in National Championships or other major matches organised by the National Federation of Anglers. Flowing rivers, such as the Trent and Severn and even the Upper Thames, where LAA clubs rarely ventured, saw the competitions on them dominated by float fishing and on the slower, deeper rivers and drains like the Huntspill and Great Ouse, groundbait had to be thrown by hand. Even for loose feeding, catapults and throwing sticks were forbidden and everything had to be hand-thrown.

There were some weird and wonderful tricks attempted and I recall an angler being disqualified on the Norfolk Broads National in the mid-1960s for using a rolled-up newspaper to throw maggots as feed!

It was soon after the creation of what became the conventional blockend

The best excuse for loafing in the countryside

feeder that I was invited to become a founder-member of a new match-orientated fishing club, the Terrapins who used the blockend to devastating effect. The club entered a team into the LAA Challenge Shield at a time when fishing in London and the south was on a real upswing. The LAA was growing and match fishing, as against competitive club angling, was growing in popularity.

It was dace that the blockend caught on the Thames: they homed in, sometimes on the splash as the feeder hit the water, as they had never been fished for in the middle of the river before, only close in by anglers float fishing under their rod tips. Even some swims that had never seen an angler, because of really shallow water close in, had access to deeper water flowing over a gravel bottom further out and dace were there. And we were the only people with the blockend, apart from Twiggy.

The Shield is a knockout competition organised in a similar fashion to the FA Cup: all the teams went into a draw and teams drawn to fish against each other, one against one. Then another draw was made to find the venue they were to fish and these venues included much of the Lower Thames, from Richmond right upstream to Goring in Oxfordshire. There were also a few venues on the River Lea, at Wormley, Rye House and St Margaret's.

The first year Terrapins entered the Shield we were forced to fish a match in a pre-qualifying round and when our name came out of the hat alongside a team highly experienced in the Sheild, London Transport Angling Society, some of our members were hoping to exhibit their new-found weapon. As for Billy and me, we were two that didn't enjoy fishing with the blockend: it was a means to an end, if you'll forgive the pun, and that end was usually a bag of dace. We preferred our float fishing and the mixture of roach and dace that could bring. When the venue draw placed us at Wormley, on the River

Lea, where the effect of the blockend was neutralised by several factors, not least of which was no dace, we were suddenly struggling to find a team of six anglers that fancied it, especially as our opponents were recognised as a team of float anglers that enjoyed using hemp as bait and the Lea was known as a hemp venue. Luckily Billy and I had fished the Lea for most of our lives, we even fished Wormley quite regularly in summer after work. Not only was that in our favour but, as it was very early season, hemp wouldn't be the threat it could be a few weeks later in the summer. This was also to be Graham Blake's first match ever. Blakey had fished the Lea but we were slightly concerned on the morning of the match when it appeared he would be pinning his hopes on catching with cheese paste, hardly bait for summer competitions. As it was, with our maggot and caster tactics and despite Blakey's cheese, we managed to beat LT by 14 fish to 10 – yes that's just 24 sizeable fish between 12 anglers in an eight hour match: fishing wasn't as easy as some remember!

What we needed next was a draw on the Thames and we got it, not against easy opponents either. The Walthamstow Brothers had won the Shield previously, albeit several years earlier, and were an experienced outfit. The venue draw was Walton on Thames, from the bridge through the straight section cut in the 1950s to save boats travelling all the way round the long Halliford Bend, known as the Desborough Cut. This narrow piece of river carries much of the flow, making it perfect blockend water. We were slightly short of 'talent' due to holidays but our team of six was Billy Allen, Billy Harris, Johnny Wade, Micky Lambert, one of Wadey's mates called Bonner and me. I had opted to float fish in an attempt to catch some of the quality roach that lived, and still live, in the Desborough Cut. There was also the risk that barbel could discount several dace, although the blockend caught some of those too.

The match is fished as a 'walk-off', where a coin-toss at the start decides which team has the first member walk off to choose a swim. The remaining anglers then move off at 10 second intervals. We knew a good swim for barbel so Bonner and Micky Lambert were designated to hold that area while the rest of us spread along the Cut. A referee is appointed to each round and has the duty of walking the length, ensuring rules are being kept and also to conduct three 'counts' during the day, asking each angler how many sizeable fish were in their keepnet.

At the first count I had one roach so when the referee told me we had 40-odd fish already, it was obvious that my choice of float fishing was probably not the right one. When he told me that our opponents had just one single fish between the six of them it was even more obvious! Time for me to relax. I strolled down to where Micky and Bonner were fishing to learn that not only were we dominating the scoring but that Bonner and Micky both had a barbel of 5 pounds or so, plus dace. Billy H was catching dace almost at will, as was Billy A so I sat down with him for a cup of tea and one of the cakes he always took with him. We were not under much threat. As I strolled back towards my swim, I saw a member of the opposition playing a big fish, obviously a barbel. As we were under no pressure and I have never been one to miss the chance of a little bit of winding-up, I asked if I could get the landing net for him. He rebuffed my assistance and, whilst I watched, he netted the fish, as I suspected, a barbel. The captors have the choice to have any big fish weighed at once so I asked him if he'd like me to find the referee, which I did and the fish was called at 6 pounds 7 ounces, a very decent fish indeed. The angler, obviously not averse to a gloat himself, said: "That will knock a few of your dace out, won't it." He was somewhat deflated to learn that two of our first count also included barbel.

After a further hour float fishing with no more fish I decided to swap to the blockend and, despite the very heavy river traffic, the fish were there and it wasn't long before I was enjoying the fun too.

The final score was 119 fish, including three barbel, eight roach and 108 dace, to Terrapins'; three fish; two dace and that single barbel to the very experienced Walthamstow Brothers. The blockend was born!

Eventually the secret was released into the public domain. Anglers knew how we were catching but had no idea of the construction of the feeders, as we hadn't with Twiggy's. A couple of poor imitations were made and, once they became popular, anglers started to catch well, even on such bad designs, so much so that the mighty London Anglers Association called an Emergency General Meeting to ban: 'The infernal machines', as then-chairman Reg Cooke described them. The motion was defeated. I was fishing the Thames at Staines one day when John Gladwin, of the famous London angling family whose fame is now carried by Derek Gladwin, asked how they worked. To save messing about I gave him an original and within a few months Thamesley Tackle had produced an excellent version that changed the face of angling, match fishing in particular, forever.

Keith Arthur

The Terrapins

The Terrapins was a fishing club with a difference. Founded in September 1966 from an idea by Johnny Wade it evolved over the years and at one time was one of the most feared match teams in the country. It didn't start like that!

I was one of the founder members of which there were 12 in all. Wadey arranged enamelled badges for us; just 12 were made and I still have mine in my 'Important Medals' box. Most of the members lived in Dalston in East London and although I had worked in Hackney, right next door, for a few years, I was a bit of an outsider, along with my pal Billy Allen who, at that time, had never fished a single competition. And competitions were why the club was formed with the LAA Shield as our ultimate goal. Although we had some fabulous matches and travelled much of England to fish them, the first Terrapin incarnation was based around a group of like-minded men having a very good time at the waterside.

Wadey was the leader and, as I have explained previously, ran a West Indian fruit and vegetable stall in Ridley Road market, as did Micky Lambert, his best mate. Although they were technically competing with one another for business they did most things together, especially fish. Micky Lambert didn't (and still doesn't!) drive so he was Wadey's travelling companion. Both were similar stature; very large and both enjoyed laughing as much as they did fishing. Micky was a better joke teller than Wadey too because at the very least he reached the end without collapsing into a heap. Even if the joke wasn't hilarious it was as well to laugh or else a 'nip' was on the cards. A 'nip' entailed Micky pinching and lifting a piece of skin and flesh inside the bicep of anyone who offended him. It was almost levitation and we all, at some time, had big bruises to explain away.

Billy Harris was another founder member; the man responsible for the lead used on the blockend feeders and for, single-handedly, reducing the amount of copper under the streets of East London. Most of it found its way to scrap yards, illegally of course and, bearing that in mind in conjunction with his pretty frugal ways, resulted in him walking into a bemused estate agents with more than £40,000 in cash to buy a house near his beloved River Waveney in Norfolk. He didn't live long enough to enjoy his life there, which is a real tragedy.

Bill had a great way with words, mixing and confusing metaphors in a way so that, on first hearing, they sounded correct. On a Shield match at Staines I was sitting with him when he landed a 'goer' and, as he slid it into his keepnet, said: "That's another coffin in their nail." On days when the Thames would be whipped up by a strong upstream breeze, creating what River Trent anglers call 'upgate rollers', Billy would suggest there was: "… too much water on the wind." He was also a stroke-puller of the first order and if he could bend the odd rule, he did. One of our regular match venues was the River Cam outside Cambridge. The organising club banned hempseed as bait and, as usual when something is banned, the assumption is that it works. So Bill used to take a pint of cooked hemp, secreted in one of his Barbour coat pockets and selected a swim out of main view, between two bushes for example. Whilst tackling up he would take advantage of any passing boat or gust of wind to throw in a handful of the banned seed, coughing loudly to disguise the splash. I only recall it ever working on one occasion when Bill finished joint third in the match, although whether this was because of the hemp or in spite of it, we will never know.

At the time of the Terrapins, Bill was living in a semi-basement flat in Dalston with his dogs Sam. That isn't a typo: Bill had several golden Labradors, one at a time, during the years that I knew him, all called Sam. It provided some kind of continuity I suppose. Although he lived in what in many peoples' terms would be described as squalor he never went without and nor did Sam. When Bill got out of bed, Sam got in. What Bill ate, Sam ate. He would always have a fridge-full of food including a big chunk of home-cooked boiled bacon from which he'd hack some pieces for one of his legendary salad sandwiches. These comprised of two slices, cut like doorsteps, from a bloomer loaf, spread with butter then half an inch or so of the bacon. Lettuce and tomato would be added then slices of beetroot. The overall dimensions were impressive, getting on for 3 inches thick. This would be cut in half and packed in a brown paper bag, as used on Wadey's market stall.

Micky Herbert was another member who, for reasons I can't explain, was known as 'Darby'. Darby was a refugee from the strict discipline of the Tamesis, always on the fringes of their team but good enough for ours. He worked in the building trade but soon after joining took 'The Knowledge' and became a London cab driver, a job which seemed to suit his laconic demeanour to the hilt. He is another naturally very funny bloke, fiercely patriotic. I can never forget the times we travelled together and as anglers we do get to see some wonderful places, often with staggering views over valleys. Darby would never fail to point them out, saying: "Look at that! That's

England that is. Why anyone wants to go abroad does my head in." His other regular remark on the way home was: "If my dinner ain't on the table when I get in, I'm gonna get nasty. And if it is, I'm gonna tip it all over 'er." Of course that never happened but it always drew a chuckle.

Graham Blake was also introduced to competitive fishing by joining us. Here was a man who was, and still is, funny without trying, or intending to be. He rarely appeared happy and if pessimists are described as having a glass that is half-empty, Blakey's glass was cracked too. He is a remarkably talented, natural angler who catches more than his fair share of fish and also has the happy talent of drawing very well. In match fishing 'the draw' is where anglers pick a piece of paper or counter from bag or box. On that will be a number designating the spot to be fished from. Blakey always denied his ability at the drawbag but, as an example, I was recently walking along a dockside in Florida with Billy Allen. In one spot, between two moored boats, a huge shoal of fish were milling about, as fish do, for no apparent reason. Bill just looked down, looked back up at me and said: "Blakey's peg." And we both knew exactly what he meant.

The other main component of our match team was Johnny Worth, a tall, gangly character who was the practical joker of the party. Many times we'd pull up at a set of traffic lights on the way home from a match, or just a team session, and Worthy would pick up someone's shoes – we'd usually ride home in the boots we'd worn fishing rather than change back into our morning footwear, often carpet slippers, – open the back door of the minibus and throw them out. The unlucky victim then had to get out, retrieve their shoes and run back to where we'd been able to stop. As they reached for the door it was always a case of just pulling forward that few yards more. Usually Wadey would be driving so he was immune, as was Micky Lambert who was too big to pick on and had the 'nip' as a form of retaliation.

Amazingly we were also pretty good at match fishing, in our many and varied ways, and this was a time when the match scene was beginning to take off in the south-east. The rest of the country had been fishing 'open' matches, where anyone can enter, for generations but in London we had just two on the Lower Thames: the Hammersmith Open, fished as a roving match in sections from Kingston Bridge to Walton and often attracting an entry of more than 800 anglers, and the Southwark Open, fished from Windsor Bridge to Boveney Lock. The Southwark was limited to 400 entries and how all those squeezed in – it always sold out – is anyone's guess.

Wadey was desperately unlucky not to win one of the major LAA matches: the Thames Benevolent Trophy. The match was fished between Walton and Kingston and Wadey drew the Walton section, choosing a swim near the 'Chinese bridge' on a narrow section opposite D'Oyly Carte Island. The river has good pace and perfect depth here, with 'cabbages' on the nearside shelf, dropping to a clean, gravel bottom around 8-9 feet deep down the central channel. The far bank is piled, with 4 feet of water close to the bank. Wadey had the still-exclusive blockend tactics and at the end of the match had four barbel in his net. Single barbel appeared quite regularly, pairs rarely and four was just about unheard of. When the scales arrived John put the fish on one at a time and the largest bumped the scales right down to their 8 pound limit. Each club had to provide a steward on the day and one of those was allocated the job of scalesman, accompanied by another whose job was to record the weights. This was the first time in anyone's experience that a scale had been bottomed. Only one set of scales was allocated to a section so there was no opportunity to hang the fish, in the weigh sling, between two balances so the steward called the weight at 8 pounds although it was obviously considerably more. He would not even move on the suggestion that the needle had gone past the 8 pounds mark and was sitting on 12 ounces on a second revolution, and with a gap between the 8 pounds and 0 pounds it had to be at least an extra pound.

Despite much arguing, the stewards wouldn't budge so the weight of 8 pounds was allocated and although it didn't make a jot of difference to the individual result – Wadey won the match – on the team score we were beaten by just 4 ounces. This made the news in the angling press in a big way and drew the attention of one angling journalist in particular. Keith Elliott was working freelance for one of the fishing weeklies as well as his local Maidenhead paper and was intrigued by the catch – four barbel on a Thames match simply didn't happen – and contacted John to find out how he had caught them. The blockend had received no publicity thus far but it was about to happen! Keith asked if we could make an attempt to replicate Wadey's feat in front of his camera and, naturally, we agreed.

We returned to the site of Wadey's triumph: John himself, Big Micky, Worthy, Billy Harris and me. It was a very warm, early autumn day as we spread ourselves out over the area from opposite the downstream end of the island up to the Chinese bridge. And, as often happens, the fish simply didn't play ball. We were even struggling to catch dace which, on better days, would frequently attack the feeder as soon as it hit the water, following it down to the bottom eating the maggots as they were forced by pressure of water through the holes. This day everything was dead. Worthy eventually caught a barbel, to this day the smallest I have ever seen from the Thames, no more than 7 inches long or a couple of ounces in weight.

Mr Elliott was wondering how he could forge a piece of creative journalism from what was happening when the cry went up: "Here you go,

I've got a 'big chap.'" Billy Harris was in to a barbel, referred to by him as 'big chaps' every time he caught one. Then, disaster! The fish snagged in mid-river. Bill used appreciable gear but even on his salmon spinning rod and Bell nylon (like wire!) he could not move the fish. He swore he could feel it so Wadey took action. Removing his shirt, exposing his massive bulk to the elements as well as some unsuspecting lady scullers, he dived straight in! A powerful breast stroke soon saw him mid-river, directly over the snag and, with Bill's line in his hand, he performed what I was told during life-saving classes at school swimming lessons was known as a duck dive. Masses of bubbles burst on the surface, followed by some twigs that were attached to a larger branch that surfaced, like Excalibur, from the water in Wadey's hand. Suspended from one of the branches was Bill's blockend and, 4 inches below it, on the hook, a dace of maybe 6 inches; scarcely a big chap!

Wadey carried the lot to the bank and climbed up the sandbag bank, the little fish was unhooked and released to grow bigger while John looked for his clothes which had, mysteriously gone missing. In any similar circumstance there was always one culprit, the man who tossed shoes from moving minibuses: Worthy. He was standing slightly away from the group with his back turned, his thin shoulders rising and falling as he attempted to hide his mirth. Showing a surprising turn of speed – Wadey was no mean footballer and had been a very good competitive swimmer before growing to his then-current size – he caught Worthy, all 6 foot 2 inches and 10 stone dripping wet of him, and launched him, almost javelin fashion, into the river. I don't ever recall laughing so hard in an angling environment: tears of laughter were rolling down my face and my ribs were hurting – until I was committed to the river too. Keith Elliott may not have got his blockend 'scoop' but his camera was busy clicking and although I have never seen the pictures myself, he assures me he still has them somewhere. As editor of *Classic Angling* magazine, maybe one day they will surface because, even out of context, they must be great value.

Another of my favourite Billy Harris stories also involves the 'big chaps'. One of his favourite stretches of Thames for catching barbel was the section below Boulters Lock at Maidenhead, running parallel to the main road to Cookham. Driving along the road it appears that the river is directly at the bottom of the wall, flanked by railings but there is a narrow catwalk, maybe 2½ feet wide, that is used to moor boats waiting for the lock gates to open. A hundred yards or so downstream of the lock the flow from the weir hits the bank – an area the 'big chaps' hang out in. The best swim used to be opposite a garden with steps leading to the river, flanked by lion sculptures, ironically similar to another barbel hotspot between Kingston and Hampton Court – if that's not giving a game away I don't know what is!

Thursday afternoons were our favourite time to fish there: Wadey and Micky's pitches in Ridley Road Market and the shop I worked in, Times Furnishing in Mare Street, Hackney, were forced to close for half days by the local trading laws. Billy simply filled in whatever hole we was supposed to be down, hid his LEB handcart and joined us.

Late summer was best and, despite having what Bill described as: "... too many butterflies about", his definition of fair-weather anglers and boaters, The Wall was a favourite of his. We all float fished, trotting down using a crow quill float, feeding copious amounts of maggots through a bait dropper. We would catch plenty of dace as well as a few roach and perch before the big chaps showed up and bullied them out of the way: then it was barbel city. Billy couldn't be bothered to mess around with the smaller species so he tried to deter them by using larger hooks and fishing with his bait hard on the bottom, using a drilled bullet weight to hold the bait there. Often he would finish up with a single maggot impaled on a size 6 hook, one of what he called his 'trusty rustys', kept in a Golden Virginia 2 ounce tobacco tin, the contents doused in 3-in-1 oil.

On one occasion a boat was moored near his favourite swim with someone fishing from the back. Bill ascertained that this was a hire cruiser with a family from Boston, Lincs, on their holidays. The man was used to fishing the River Witham in his home town, a very slow-flowing river compared to this narrow section of Thames, the proximity of the weir making it even faster. Bill took delight in explaining about the big chaps and how they fought, first hugging the bottom, then moving inexorably upstream against the current, testing tackle and angling skills to the limit. Bill's description wasn't as flowery but sufficiently effective to have his audience's rapt attention.

Eventually the man on the boat hooked something and that something hugged the bottom. Recalling Bill's graphic description, there was only one possible explanation in his mind: he'd hooked a barbel. In reality he'd hooked an old mooring chain that, as he pulled, lifted from the bottom then sank back down again.

"I've got one, I've got a barbel!!!" he yelled. Big Micky, ready for a micky-take, sauntered up.

"What's up mate?" he asked.

"I've got a barbel!" came the reply.

"Nah, you've hooked the bottom mate" Micky asserted. The reply, in a Lincolnshire accent, has been repeated every time Micky has told this story – and that's a fair old few I promise:

"But eet's pullingggg."

Keith Arthur

Billy was cursing as his swim was being upset by the lifting and falling of whatever was on the end of the holidaymaker's line. Wadey, Micky and I couldn't fish for laughing and the holidaymaker was becoming more and more excited until the inevitable happened and a length of old, weed-encrusted rope and chain appeared behind his cruiser.

Once things had calmed down, we resumed our fishing and Bill decided it was time for his salad sandwich. Reaching into his jacket pocket, the brown paper bag was removed and half the sandwich extracted. Bill wasn't over-blessed in the dental department, having just a couple of teeth in opposite corners of his jaw, food items travelling between the two on a sort of vacuum principle. He took a huge bite/suck at the sandwich, holding it in his left hand whilst his right was engaged holding the rod. Then, the inevitable happened and Bill's float shot under, the bite dragging the rod tip round and pulling line from the reel: Billy's big chap had turned up. His left hand, currently holding the sandwich, would be required to operate the reel so Bill took one look at the sandwich, just a single huge mouth-shaped bite missing, then he looked at the rod, the reel slowly yielding line, then looking back, almost lovingly at the sandwich, he put the rod down onto the concrete ledge, planted a size 11 LEB-issue welly on it, and continued the feast. It really was too good to waste.

Memories inspire others. Like looking for a word in a dictionary, other words are found on the way, diverting one's mind from the original target. The Terrapins were much more than Billy, much more than the sum of the parts and there are many more tales to tell. Luckily I still have plenty of room. Read on.

Keith Arthur

Alec's Hat and other Adventures

Through the years fishing around the south of England and beyond with Terrapins we had a few funny moments, most of which, as you would expect, revolving around the misfortune of one member or another. Some members, or guests, seemed more prone to disaster than others and Old Alec was one of those.

Alec was a retired window cleaner who used some words and phrases even I had never encountered before, and I had worked with a porter at Times Furnishing in Holloway who was always coming out with rhyming slang, backslang and other spoken, yet alien, forms of communication. Alec simply used different words, the most popular one was 'jillpots', delivered as an insult. I have always assumed that this would be spelt '*gill*pots' as in the old liquid measure of a quarter-pint,and meant that, in pint terms, the receptor of the insult wasn't all there.

He also had the great Richard Walker as a hero and after a bad day where he had failed to catch much (most days) he would comment on how Dick Walker would have done in the same swim. He introduced me to a phrase I have used regularly to date, describing an angler who had sat in a 'flyer' as having to: "... hide behind a tree to put his bait on." Alec had obviously been quite a 'ginga' in his younger days and the hair that remained on his head still carried a distinct 'strawberry blonde' look. On top of it Alec perched a baggy cheesecutter cap in red tartan. He would have mixed in well at, say, Hampden Park, Glasgow.

One of Alec's traits was to wander away from where the rest of us would be fishing then, at the end of the day, stroll back with tales of super roach and dace and, quite often some monster of the deep hooked and lost. Rarely, if ever, were these captures witnessed. An example was a trip to Staines on a day when the fishing was best described as 'testing'; it was tough to get a bite. I had chosen a swim on the 'Silver Sands', a bend in the river a few hundred yards upstream of Penton Hook Weir. The Sands can be a superb area for catching roach in winter and on this autumn day I had managed to catch seven of them plus a dace. The river was clear, with little flow and I had noticed, lying in the edge trapped in some reeds, a dead roach of maybe 10 ounces.

As this was a practice day and I had found a few fish, I decided to try further round the bend, in amongst some overhanging willows, towards where the rest of the team were. Alec had seen me move and announced that he was going to try the spot I had just left using a feeder, as I had caught my fish on the float.

A couple of hours, and not many fish later, it was time for home and as we walked back towards Alec, on route to Wheatsheaf Lane and our transport, Alec bent down and picked up a fish, waving it in the air, shouting: "I only had the one, nice roach though." He then proceeded to toss the plainly dead fish as far as possible into the flow. On the way home he was full of how it had been a gentle bite but had fought hard when it was obvious he'd simply picked up the dead'un.

On another practice occasion we had travelled to Tilehurst, upstream of Reading and, yet again, the fishing was poor. Most of us were fishing downstream of Scours Lane, the entry to the river, where a small stream enters. Alec had been telling us stories of missed bites and chewed maggots but, apart from the odd bleak, little had been caught so, when Alec went for a walk, leaving his tackle unattended, I went into the stream behind and netted a few minnows. Winding in Alec's gear, Worthy took the top off his feeder and put two minnows inside before closing it and recasting.

Several minutes later Alec returned to tell us that nothing was being caught, picked up his rod and reeled in.

"Look at THAT!" he said. "Greedy little jillpotses. I told you I was getting bites, they've only squeezed through the holes in me feeder and ate me maggots then got too fat to get out again."

But Alec's greatest moment came at Tovil, on the River Medway. This is quite a deep, slow-flowing stretch of river, upstream of Maidstone. Ten of us were spread out along the river, from the bridge upstream, where bushes and trees make each swim fairly secluded. Wadey was closest to the bridge, then Micky, then Alec. Sport wasn't great – to be fair most of the time it wasn't – but the day was pleasant enough.

Suddenly Micky spied something floating down:

"Oy, Wadey, that looks like Alec's hat," he said.

"It is. I wonder what the silly old sod's done now?" replied John.

"Oy, Wadey! That looks like Alec," said Micky because there he was, drifting downstream, treading water.

Now bear in mind that Alec was not a young man but, I suppose, a lifetime of climbing ladders, bucket in hand, had given him a degree of fitness... or maybe it was just panic keeping him up there. Luckily he was still very close to the bank as the river banks are pretty sheer into 4-5 feet of water.

"Help!" cried Alec. "Get me out!"

By now Wadey was involved and was holding out his landing net, with an 8 foot long extending metal handle. Alec grasped the net and Wadey slowly pulled him towards dry land. Of course it would have been impossible to lift Alec out but, in true drowning man/straw fashion, he refused to let go of the net and take Micky's outstretched hand. A couple more of us had walked down to see what was happening and, as the situation was clearly in hand and everyone out of danger, the humour of events got the better of us. We were, mostly, lying on the bank, or rolling around in the grass, laughing uncontrollably. This got worse when Wadey exclaimed:

"Alec, let go mate. It's a new handle I don't want it to get bent."

"GET BENT! I'M DROWNING HERE YOU JILLPOTS," came the response and that was it. No one could move for laughing. Alec transferred his grip to an overhanging shrub, found his feet and was, somehow, pulled from the water.

Amazingly we had very few falling-in situations but one on a Shield match stays in my mind, mostly because it was me who got wet! One of the unique facets of Shield fishing was that anglers could offer assistance to team-mates to land fish and wielding the landing net when a big fish was hooked was commonplace. We had drawn a team called Negretti and Zambra, formed from workers at the world-famous instrument makers, on the Thames at Bray. The river was carrying some extra water and, as this narrow section of the river is directly below a weir, was hacking along at a fair old lick.

The swims are mostly on sheer bank, 4 feet or so above the water, and at least 3 feet next to the bank, which is lined with thorny bushes, many of them dog-rose. I was fishing upstream of Billy Allen when he hooked a barbel and, characteristic of this hard-fighting fish, it made its way upstream, heading into the flow. Bill called out so I grabbed my landing net and walked down to his aid. The fish was about 5 yards upstream of Bill, quite close in and he had managed to get it off the bottom. Once this happens barbel are not quite as powerful and I thought it was ready for the net. All I could see in the coloured water was the tip of the fish's tail; its head was still down. Reaching out as far as I could, I was still an agonising couple of feet short of the fish so taking a grip on a shrub, I stepped onto a tiny piece of bank I could just make out on the waterline... only it wasn't bank but a little raft of flotsam carried down by the rising river.

That put me up to my waist in very cold Thames, still hanging on to the flimsy shrub, with the barbel, luckily remaining firmly attached to Bill's line, now headed back out to midstream.

"I think you're meant to net it, not ride it," was the not-unexpected comment from 'my pal' who was playing the fish. I managed to struggle out of the water and, in the finest tradition of 'all's well that ends well' we won the match 47-4.

Anyway, it's not as if Mr Allen was immune from taking the early bath. Bill's wife Carol used to come fishing with us some evenings after work, her favourite venue being the River Lea at Wormley. Bill used to set up with Carol between us so if one of us was busy when she hooked the inevitable big fish, the other could assist with the landing net. One particular evening the weather was not playing the game, with clouds and rain on and off. Carol was in her usual spot, between Bill and I, but she then decided she needed to be in Bill's swim. A rod rest was always positioned for Carol, so she could put the rod on it and watch the float, lifting the rod to strike and, with the banks being piled along this stretch of River Lea, the rod rest needed to be at least 4 feet long, to stick into the riverbed.

Fishing

Keith Arthur

Bill moved the umbrella first, then Carol's chair and next came the rod rest. The margins of the river here are mostly clay: tough, clingy clay at that and Bill had to really tug and pull to remove it. Eventually it gave, Bill almost falling backwards when his pressure told. He walked the few yards to where Carol was sitting, tutting away whilst waiting to fish. Bill lifted the rod rest over his head, as if he was wielding a massive club, and stabbed it riverwards. Unfortunately the water was at least a foot deeper than in the initial spot and Bill went tumbling, base over apex, into the water. To give him full credit, he got out even faster than he went in, the only signs of entry being one Barbour jacket pocket full of River Lea water. No one said a word.

On reflection, maybe I should keep away from venues beginning with 'B' as I have fallen in twice more, at Bourne End and Boveney. The first time, at Boveney was awful: a cold, January day and a long walk from the car park. I was fishing a Maidenhead and District AA match and had drawn on the wooded area downstream of Queen's Island, below the good pegs on the White House. The water was shallow, both close in and further out and, in company with every other angler, I had climbed down the sheer mud bank to stand in the water and fish from there. That meant wearing waders and wearing waders meant cold, numb feet. Compared to modern angling clothing I was virtually naked, with a pair of long johns under my jeans that were, at the time, a fashionable pink shade. Yes, for fishing and yes real men wear pink. The fishing was tough and with size limits still in force I had a few roach and dace in my net. Chris Love was pegged downstream of me and he had less fish but he had caught a bonus 'scraper' chub (just over the minimum 12-inch size limit for that species).

I recall hooking a snag and losing the hook length, which entailed clambering up the bank for a replacement. There are several things I will never be and have never been: amongst those are nimble and a good climber. I had a few rat holes to aid me climb the above head-high bank and the left foot went in like a dream. The right foot went into the next hole and, being unable to feel my feet, promptly came out again, dumping me on my back in a foot or so of VERY cold water. I struggled manfully on, tying on the new hook, and adding another roach to my bag. At the weigh-in my catch was beaten by Chris Love's bag, including that chub, by a quarter of an ounce, sufficient to take the £10 section prize. All I had to do was pack up and walk the mile-plus back to Boveney Church and the warmth of my car.

By the time I reached there I was walking like John Wayne after a particularly long horse ride. My jeans rubbing and counter-rubbing with the long johns had given me chapped inner thighs, so red they glowed in the dark! Now the almost essential use of waterproof overtrousers keeps the very worst of the wet off, even in such disasters although I do my very best not to test their efficiency.

The other dunking came at Bourne End on a Woodbine qualifier. This event, sponsored by the cigarette company, was highly thought of and the first qualifier was followed by a regional final, the qualifiers from that going on to a final in Denmark and, in those days, Denmark was a brilliant destination with massive roach and bream catches from the River Guden, the highlight.

My peg was, once again, a fair old toby (walk), from Spade Oak Ferry car park to just below the big island, towards Marlow. It was high summer (for a change!) so not bad weather for taking an unplanned dip. I had decided to fish the feeder as the area I had drawn wasn't a noted spot for roach but bream sometimes hung about there. The boat traffic was heavy and, when I tried to adjust my rod rest, making the rod tip lower to push the line below the waves caused by boat-wash, I stepped onto a slippery bit and fell into, thankfully, the shallow margin. Being such a lovely day I peeled off my clothes, right down to my underpants, spreading the wet things on a convenient barbed-wire fence to dry in the sun. I took a bit of stick from passing craft – why, I can't imagine – but I did catch that bream and it was enough to qualify for the regional final.

As well as the Thames we would often have club outings to the River Ouse and found a few out-of-the-way reaches that were virtually devoid of anglers. Whether we were allowed to fish there is anyone's guess but we were never challenged. One such section was at Needingworth that even had the blessing of a pub on the bank: The Pike and Eel. This is now a hotel with a marina for the best part of 200 boats but 40 years ago was simply a pub by the river. It had a huge car park though, which was very handy, and the landlord didn't mind us using it at all as we would stop for refreshment at the end of the day, although occasionally it wasn't unknown for one or two to pause earlier. The pub dog was a St Bernard, not very old and with no brakes. As we pulled up it would lumber into the car park making those great 'woofs' that only big dogs can make, sounding like they came from the very bottom of a volcano. It would cavort and gambol about until we had loaded baskets on our back and rod holdalls over our shoulders; then it would play skittles, running at one of us full-tilt and, because of the aforementioned lack of stopping power, would simply bowl us over then lick our faces to make sure we weren't dead. The only thing lacking was the brandy barrel round its neck. It was a great dog.

It was a decent stretch of river too with some cracking roach and occasional bream which we mostly caught float fishing. It was the scene of a classic Blakey moment as when we arrived a strong downstream wind was obviously going to make bait presentation to the fish very difficult. Blakey said: "Where's the nearest bridge?"

Thinking he wanted some shelter from the wind, and not knowing the correct answer, I suggested he look upstream towards Fen Drayton.

"No, it don't matter," he said. "I was only going to fish the other bank so the wind would be upstream." Ahem.

The last time I went there, which was a very long time ago, the river authorities had been down with their dredgers and bank destroyers, removing all the foliage and shrubbery from 'our' bank, leaving a 45°, 8 foot slope of soft mud down to the water's edge. It looked awful but, as we'd travelled 60-odd miles to fish, fish we would!

It wasn't too much of a task to 'tread down' an area to place our baskets close to the water, using them as platforms for our bait allowing us to stand and fish. The river was in good nick – no need to cross to the other bank – and we were soon catching fish. It wasn't long before we were joined by a herd of cattle of the black and white Friesian variety. They were as aghast of the bank as we were, their 'cattle-drink', an area on all grazing land next to rivers where the beasts regularly go to slake their thirst, had gone. They milled about, mooing, at the top of the bank before one of them, a really brave cow, decided to, literally, take the plunge about 15 yards above where Micky Herbert (Darby) was fishing. It half slid, half stumbled down the bank but the severity of the slope caused it to keep going until it reached the natural gravel bed of the river, by which time it was way past its udders. It continued downstream, not quite panicking but equally not happy, until it reached where Micky was putting together a decent net of roach.

Although he is a VERY funny man, Darby doesn't always look it. He was once described as: "... having a face like the Idris Lemon" and those of you squash drinkers from the 60s and 70s will know exactly what I mean. Imagine a lemon, on its side, with a laconic smile and you have it. He was concerned, not only at the bovine intrusion into his Sunday pleasure, but also at how the beast was going to get out of the water. He offered it, Alec-style, a landing net to hold on to but cows aren't necessarily aware of the properties of nets. He tried 'shooing' and 'come on then'-ing and even attempted to get his landing net over the cow's head to pull it out.

With that, the creature managed to turn round then lifted its tail and, using every muscle available to it, blasted Darby and his tackle with a 60mph cowpat. This may be slightly graphic but I can tell you that cowpats don't come out round; they come out long, thin and very wet, as well as pretty hot. It was one of the funniest sights I have ever seen, even by Terrapin standards, and I can see it now as clearly as the day it happened.

There was a happy ending: the cow got out, Darby survived and we never returned. Loafing in the countryside is better with bushes and trees and NOT steep gradients – or incontinent cattle.

Great Ouse Tales

The Great Ouse featured regularly on the agenda of anglers from North London. The LAA held the fishing rights on many miles of the river from downstream of Bedford to the Denver in Norfolk, during which journey the river goes through several dramatic changes of character.

I had read all about the Great Ouse, especially the great bream catches from Littleport, downstream of Ely in the Fens, where the river has been deepened and widened. My school pal, Derek Reeve, suggested we should go there and his father Charles, an extremely elegant man, took us in his lovely car that I believe was a Wolseley. It was big, with leather seats, that is certain. He dropped us at a bridge almost opposite the sugar beet factory – I remember the sign for Prickwillow (well, wouldn't you when you were at school?) – and we caught some small roach and skimmer bream float fishing in the deep margins. A competition was taking place on the other bank, I think it was a club from Sheffield, and they weren't catching much, in fact we could hear their comments about: "... bloody kids are catching on't far side."

Once again, the writings of Richard Walker were on our minds and stories of Great Ouse monsters which, he believed, could quite possibly be wels catfish as no other fish were big enough to fight the way they did. Of course, if anyone was going to catch one of these mythical beasts, it may as well be me, so out came the trusty split cane rod granddad's will had funded and two large lobworm were mounted on a big hook. A coffin weight would keep the bait firmly on the bottom in the very slow flow and I cast the rod out as a 'sleeper', left to fish for itself. It was only the sound of it dragging along the concrete bridge pier that alerted me to the fact that I had a bite and when I struck, the rod took on a fair old curve, well into pike territory at least. The fish slowly made its way downstream and I followed for maybe 50 yards. It then turned and made its way back up towards the bridge and I was certain I had done what Walker couldn't do: catch a Great Ouse catfish! Unfortunately the hook eventually fell out of the fish and its identity remains a mystery. If I had to make a guess at the species it would be pike, carp or big eel because there was no spectacular action, just a constant powerful run. The only fish I have ever hooked that felt similar was on the Thames at Medley and I never saw that one either! Who knows: it *might* have been a catfish.

My next Ouse encounter came with the North London Angling Society, the one that met at The Old Crown, owned by my pal Brian's parents. The club held the fishing rights, and access to, Willow Tree Island at Offord Cluny and I broke my Great Ouse duck there on a club outing. The island was reached by means of a floating wooden pontoon, secured to each bank and operated by pulling a rope with pulleys on either end. It was a slightly unstable affair, especially when laden with a few anglers and tackle but, as far as I know, it never suffered a failure.

The island is on a bend in the river where the main stream is divided, not only by the island but forms into a fairly complicated set of backwaters and meanders with the main stream leading to Offord Weir on one side and a smaller branch on the other. The fishing was not bad, with roach and dace prevalent, along with some perch, chub, bream and pike and legering with maggots could guarantee a bootlace eel virtually every cast. Of course eels didn't count in matches, not LAA club-run ones anyway.

The club constructed a big shed in the middle of the island and made it available for anglers to stay in and Brian decided we should have a stay there. In those days I was far less demanding of creature comforts and would quite happily sleep in a tent or, in this case a big garden shed, if there was the chance of some fishing. There was no electricity, all cooking and lighting was by portable gas and thinking back how we survived without TV, radio or a telephone is unbelievable but, in reality, we didn't have much in the way of telly to watch at home, even with all two available channels! And radio, Sunday lunchtimes excepted, was just as dire. The chances are not many people we knew had phones either so making our own entertainment, which involved sleeping, fishing, eating and sleeping again was simple.

Night fishing has never been a forte of mine: the first time I tried it was a first night of the season effort at the North Met Pit at Cheshunt. I was still at school and a small group of us went. It didn't take long to find out we had omitted to bring any water so we simply took some from the pit to make our tea and it wasn't until morning that we discovered that every single cupful had small things swimming around in it; mostly daphnia. I suppose boiling the water made them not dangerous – maybe even edible – but it isn't something I would advise, or try again for that matter.

So one thing we made sure of was plenty of water, along with the tinned goods we'd be living on, after all the important thing was the fishing. We caught some bream, mostly at first light with the occasional one at dusk. We caught some eels whilst trying to catch bream so set out on an eel-catching mission. Knowing that big eels eat fish and scavenge for food, a dead fish seemed the perfect bait and I had read somewhere (if only I had learned as much from my school text books) that gudgeon were an excellent bait and as luck would have it, they were present in abundance.

On the first attempt, at night when eels fed best, we set up leger rigs with a dead gudgeon mounted on a size 8 hook, cast out and, in best Heath Robinson style, set up bite alarms by balancing a penny on the rim of an empty Nescafe tin, held there by the line. If the line tightened or slackened, the penny dropped! We must have missed half a dozen bites, all resulting in a gudgeon with a munched head. The eels were taking them headfirst and although we had hooked the dead fish through the lips, somehow the eels managed to avoid the hooks. Our next move was to thread the hook length through the gudgeon from the mouth to the vent – bum for non-anglers – so the hook rested in the mouth and couldn't fail to be at the correct angle to nail the fish when it ran with the bait. We caught a couple of eels but I think that most of the takes were from the very same bootlace-sized examples we were catching on maggots.

Fishing was slow during the day so we decided to fish the weir pool, reached by crossing on the pontoon to the 'mainland'. It was a beautiful overflow weir, using a spillway rather than gates so as the river rose more water flowed over. The water travelled from the weir towards the road bridge and as the pool narrowed it flowed between banks of reeds – the dark-green variety I call bream sticks, as bream, nor barbel for that matter, were far away from them on the Thames. Another great method I had read about but never attempted was fishing with silkweed. This plant grows on weir sills, lying on the slope like green lace curtains and legend has it that roach in particular, as well as dace and chub, hang about below the sill waiting for strands to break off. The method was to run a bare hook through the weed without touching it by hand then trotting it through the faster water. The plant is so fragile that finger pressure can damage it sufficiently to make it less appealing to the hungry fishes waiting its arrival. Almost unbelievably, first cast the float went under and I caught a roach, a feat I repeated many times. Brian joined in until one of his roach was taken by a small pike as he was playing it in.

Twenty minutes later he was back with his pike rod, collected from our hut on the island, complete with wire trace and treble hooks. Impaling a live roach through the back, he cast it into the flow and waited for the pike to make a fatal mistake – and it wasn't long in doing so as Brian's pike float bobbled across the top, stopped, then took off again. A firm strike resulted in a severely bent rod and line being taken from his reel at a rate of knots. One thing was for sure, if this was a pike it wasn't the one that had snaffled his roach on the silkweed: it was a whole lot bigger.

The fight went on for some time until the line parted above the wire trace and, having read the same stories as me, Brian immediately suggested he had hooked one of Walker's catfish too. And maybe he had.

Our trip to Willow Tree Island eventually came to an end and I have only been back once to see if it looked the same. It didn't, everything looked so much smaller than I recalled, maybe because we now use roach poles that will stretch across 50 feet and more, bringing everything nearer, including perspective.

It wasn't uncommon for pike to be taken for the pot even into the 1970s and Billy Harris enjoyed eating them. He had found a place upstream of Barford Bridge where the river had a cutting from it, forming a small pool, which held lots of pike that had a liking for spinners. Bill suggested we had a day there. This was the extreme upstream point of navigation on the Ouse at the time and the river was shallow and gravel-bottomed for the most part with beds of bream sticks and cabbages which held good chub, roach and plenty of dace. None of those interested Bill, who wanted his pike.

Keith Arthur

He actually caught several, keeping one about 5 pounds, the ideal size for eating according to Mr Walker who truly was *the* angling icon of his generation. He had even published recipes for pike, and other coarse fish, in *Angling Times*. Bill gave the pike a clunk on the head with a heavy bankstick, placed it in his empty canvas bucket and off we went. On arriving at his flat, Bill took the pike and placed it in the fridge. At the time he was sharing his flat with another old friend of mine, Brian Gent, who is now a top fly angler, fishing mostly for salmon or exotic species such as striped bass and sharks with a fly rod.

When Brian got up for work the next day, Sam (the dog) was sniffing the pike which, somehow, was lying in the middle of the kitchen floor. Brian woke Bill who, taking no chances reached out with the kitchen broom and touched the fish, which responded by flicking its tail! With no more ado, Bill took his large kitchen knife and whacked the fish once more across the cranium before returning it to the cold box. Ten minutes later it had revived enough to push open the door once again. That was it, as far as Bill was concerned it had survived sufficiently to earn a permanent reprieve so he filled his not-so-well-used bath from the cold tap and dropped the pike, covered as it was with fluff and dust, into the water. A few bubbles came from its gills, which soon started moving again. I can only guess that the bashes on the head knocked the fish out temporarily and the cold dampness of the fridge created a sort of suspended animation. But it lived and needed rehousing.

Brian had a grievance with a riding school in Epping who, in their grounds, had a pond filled with small carp and goldfish. That was the eventual destination, after all they felt this fish had earned a place at the top table and would never want for a meal again. And Bill never killed another pike.

Keith Arthur

Billy Allen and I had been impressed by the flowing part of the river at Barford though and, when we both had a day off, decided to take a trip there. It was a very cold, frosty morning but the sky was clear when I picked Bill up from his flat near Finsbury Park in my Dormobile. We had agreed to be home early to go to the cinema, taking Bill's wife Carol and my then girlfriend who was going to their place after work to meet us. As it was early January and dusk came early, we'd be home in plenty of time. As if!

The journey there was trouble free; the old bus didn't go fast enough to skid, with its three-speed column change gearbox and we were able to park very near the bridge on the grass verge, although it was a fair old slope, making the van list to starboard a bit.

The swims just downstream of the pike cutting were excellent for chub and that's where we headed, the riverbank forming a sort of gravel beach. To reach there takes a walk across a typically rough water meadow which is crossed by a small stream that enters the river a hundred yards or so upstream of the bridge. Two planks across the stream form a crossing, better than trying one's luck with the marshy stream bed. Bill soon had a brace of chub, both around 2 pounds or so and I was catching some roach and dace on the float. The sky was noticeably darkening and at 10.30am the first flakes of snow fell and by 11am the far bank had disappeared thanks to a white curtain. I moved next to Bill so we could overlap our umbrellas, giving us more protection and packed my float rod away, switching to the feeder.

The snow fell for four hours and when it stopped, at 3pm, it was better than knee-deep, the field behind us white and level, with not even a sign of the stream. Packing up was a complete nightmare, with freezing, wet hands making gripping anything difficult and painful, the umbrellas, with aluminium poles being worst of all: the numbness of my hands making me yell in agony.

The snow had also frozen the brollies so rolling them up, even making them slightly smaller, was impossible. Now all we had to do was get home.

Walking back to the van was fun because we couldn't locate the crossing for the stream; the snow had filled the channel in, the water's path only being visible where the snow dipped from the billiard table flatness around it. Using the poles from our now frozen stiff umbrellas we ultimately located the planks and made it to the van. If it had been parked on the flat, we would possibly have never got it started: the wind had blown the snow away from the rear wheels where it had sat on the slope, giving us some traction. We loaded the gear and set off, the first thing we noticed was the heater wasn't working so no defrost for the windscreen.

I drove the first section, up to Tempsford Bridge and the A1, headed south and the first noticeable thing was zero traffic: not a car, van or lorry was on the road and, at coming up for 5pm on a weekday, this was astonishing. Visibility was minute; we had to continually wipe the screen until it started to freeze over, inside and out, the wipers being totally inadequate and the heater non-existent. The engine compartment was in the centre, under the dashboard and although opening it gave off some warmth, it made no impact whatsoever. The roadside wasn't there because of the depth of the snow and it wasn't even possible to tell whether we were on single or dual carriageway until a single headlamp coming straight towards us forced us to stop and the motorcyclist behind it, the only vehicle we'd seen in several miles, told us we were on the wrong side of a dual!

That did it; we swapped seats so Bill could drive while I held the sliding door open and navigated, stopping every so often to wipe the screen. How we did it I simply don't know, but we got home. Billy's Uncle Cyril drove a laundry van around North London and spent the night wrapped in other people's dirty sheets and blankets in the back of it, unable to make a hill. The old Dormobile plodded on but it was nearly 11pm when we arrived and Carol and Susan, my girlfriend, not the same Susan who is my wife today, were regally hacked off. I at least dropped her off at Manor House to get the late bus home. I don't know why I never saw her again.

It is just downstream of Barford, at the Roxton Fisheries, where my last Great Ouse story begins. It was the final day of the coarse fishing season, March 14th. The weather was good but it had been raining for weeks so if we were to fish a river, the choice had to be good or else floodwater would make it impossible. The party was the two Billys; Allen (Little Bill) and Harris (Big Bill) and me and we were back in the Dormobile. Big Bill suggested Roxton D, as this section is known to LAA anglers to this day. The entry is halfway between Tempsford and Barford bridges, on the east bank, the opposite side of the river to the A1. I stipulate that because knowledge of geography may enhance your amazement at this tale. Big Bill said that this section carried water well as the small lock above Barford would hold it back and the weir downstream would carry any extra water away. And we believed him.

Now the last day of the season used to be a pilgrimage for anglers and was the second-biggest absenteeism day of the year for English industry (hardly any coarse fishermen in Wales in those days and no close season in Scotland or Ireland), second only to June 16th, the first day. These dates have been dissipated somewhat as the close season now applies, in the main, to rivers. Because of the date we had an early start, predawn, at 5am and the clear roads helped us reach Roxton as the light strengthened. It was light enough for us to see the water, which was about 200 yards closer to where we had parked than it should have been, the river having burst its banks. In the middle distance we could see the forlorn shapes of trees rising from the brown, gushing torrent that indicated the natural path of the river. Big Bill said:

"What we'll do is tackle up here, carry our rods and bait over to the trees there and fish the slacks behind them."

Little Bill and I looked at each other, then at Big Bill and told him he was crazy if he thought we would paddle over a field that might have potholes, or worse as it stood next to a sewage treatment works, to stand thigh-deep in muddy water on the last day of the season! Paul Young, the Scottish actor who has made several angling series for the Discovery Channel gave me an acronym that suited this situation perfectly: 'NFWI' which stands for No Fish Worth It.

Big Bill's next suggestion was slightly better: "Bures, we can go to Bures. It never floods there."

Bures, for the geographically able, is near the town of Sudbury in Suffolk, and stands on the Suffolk Stour. Neither Little Bill nor I had ever fished there so we took Big Bill's assertions at face value and started the bus. Two and a half hours later we stopped on the top of a hill, looking down at Bures – well, actually we were looking down at several square miles of muddy-brown water with the odd tree, house and telegraph pole poking through it, proving that the Suffolk Stour DOES flood. So far we had travelled 130 miles and not taken a rod from the bag or tossed a maggot to its death.

"OK, Brains, where next?" said Little Bill.

"Old Windsor Lock Cut. Behind the lock it will be brilliant."

For those of you less familiar with southern Britain, Tempsford is about 60 miles from Dalston, Bures is approximately 75 miles from Tempsford and Old Windsor is 110 miles from Bures but only 35 miles from Dalston. Are you with me? Good.

The best excuse for loafing in the countryside

133

The long journey through Essex and London to Her Majesty's back garden (almost) close to Windsor Castle took in lunch and when we arrived it was possible – just – in a single swim directly below the lock gates, to wet a line so, desperate as we were, we did just that, the resulting catches being no more than a meagre few tiny, undersized dace. On the last day of the season a bonanza is what's needed, not a debacle. With not much more than an hour of daylight left, Big Bill suggested our final move, a local one, to what we knew as Blenheim Pit; a disused gravel pit close to Staines, controlled by the Blenheim club. In those days the River Colne ran in and out of the lake and Big Bill reckoned that, with the coloured water circulating in the lake, we'd get a few bites and the lateness of the hour and time of the season meant that either the club bailiffs would have finished their rounds or be fishing themselves, so we would get away with it.

Luckily the trip is no more than 7 miles and there was still sufficient daylight left to tackle up and fish. Little Bill and I sat to the left of the river entry, with Big Bill on the right. The Colne was indeed swirling in and forming a large, brown eddy in the black-looking clear water of the pit.

"Ten bob for the biggest?" asked Big Bill, sitting holding his rod, fishing with exactly the same tackle he'd used on the flooded Thames, a 'cork-on-crow' as he described his float, with a drilled bullet holding everything still on the bottom.

Little Bill and I were catching a fish a throw, small roach, dace and plenty of big bleak, but no 'goers'. Big Bill sat biteless in the encroaching gloom.

"One last cast," Big Bill said and, as the final wisp of steam from his breath, as the night air cooled everything, followed it up with: "Come on, give us yer cow's," (rhyming slang, cow's = cow's calf = half, half a quid, ten bob, now 50p.) His stiff rod, more effective for barbel, was bent and a few minutes later he slid the landing net under a bream of maybe 2 pounds, more than enough to take the money.

So, we had a last day to remember. A round trip of maybe 275 miles, all in an old Dormobile with no heater, hardly a fish to show for it but definitely one of the more memorable 'Last Days'. And I have to say, another great excuse.

Eyeballs in the Sky

The membership of the Terrapins club was pretty fluid and we accumulated some real characters to go with those already in place. During the 1970s one man in particular stood out and that was Bob the Pipe, so called because he would always be seen with a fuming chimney below his nose. The pipe, a fully bent variety, was always emitting a wonderful smell of high-quality tobacco and Bob was always emitting some wonderfully understated humour. He lived on the Isle of Dogs before it became Yuppyville, but was at heart still a merchant seaman, a profession in which he had spent most of his life.

Bob the Pipe was a fine angler, one of immense patience and guile, his speciality being quality roach. He knew the relatively unfished waters of the lower River Lea and surrounding backwaters like the back of his hand and could often put us on some wonderful fishing. One such place was the tidal section of the Lea across Hackney Marshes. The Lea divides at Lea Bridge Road, where the Lee Navigation Canal turns into the Hertford Union Canal, travelling south-east until it meets the Regents Canal and pours into Limehouse Basin. The tidal Lea twists and turns its way through Bow and Stratford until it meets the Thames almost opposite what is now the O2 Arena, once the Millennium Dome.

The first time Bob introduced me to the tidal Lea was a Christmas Eve. I arranged to pick him up and he directed me through the maze that is the eastern suburbs of London. When we reached Leyton he said to: "... turn right past the Oliver Twit." Without thinking I drove on, saw the pub and looked at the sign, noticing the missing 'S' in Twist. I laughed out loud asking how he knew the 'S' was missing. "Been gone for years," he said. That is the type of humour that I enjoy.

We reached the car park where countless thousands of footballers have parked for their weekend matches 'on the Marshes' and set off towards the river. When I saw it for the first time, I was dumbstruck. It was low tide and the banks were smelly, soft mud although clean gravel could be seen a few feet out. It was VERY shallow by the standards of what I was used to, no more than a yard deep, and hacking through at a fair old lick. The best time to fish the river was the final hour of the ebb then through low water. Once it started to rise the flow made fishing uncomfortable verging on the unfishable, especially as the river rose extremely rapidly by anything up to 7 or 8 feet, making a hasty retreat essential.

On this Christmas Eve the river looked 'sock on' as the Trent lads say, with a decent colour. My favourite style of coarse fishing is with a stick float, running the bait to the fish at close to the speed of the current. Bob told me to forget the stick and fish an albino porcupine quill or a bodied crow quill as some weight was required to slow the bait down for the fish to 'have it'. I took his advice and in less than four hours fishing I caught 43 roach and five dace for a total weight of close to 30 pounds. Every fish looked like a newly-minted coin and didn't appear to have ever seen a hook before, never mind felt one. Bob had a great net too and told me some other swims to try where there were more dace (my favourite river species) and fewer roach.

He was right about that too and I spent many happy days on that section of river until it was wiped out by a 'mystery pollution' so severe that eels climbed out of the water before dying. Every living thing in the river for a couple of miles was wiped out and, in their wisdom, the then National Rivers Authority stocked it with... GRAYLING! They were readily available as game anglers didn't want them and coarse anglers never saw them as they were usually found in rivers preserved for trout fishing. They lasted a month as, not being the sharpest tack in the piscine box, they were caught in large numbers by various groups of mostly 'travellers' and eaten. Whether that sublime roach and dace fishing returned I don't know because shortly after I married and moved to South-West London and with the Thames on my doorstep... well, you know the score.

I know that area of East London now has a huge concentration of cormorants that have destroyed the roach fishing in the Lea Navigation – 50 pounds+ nets of roach were caught in winter by Lea Bridge itself right into the 80s when the Black Plague descended upon us – so I can't imagine that it's as good as it was.

Some areas on the Lea Navigation were undergoing change as the river evolved from a working waterway, carrying goods by barge from the London Docks as far as Ware – a big flour mill used to sit on the river downstream of the town bridge – to a more recreational and leisure-based waterway. Narrowboats, powered by diesel engines, were replacing the old-fashioned Thames lighters that I used to watch being towed by horses, then tractors and, ultimately, barges and fancy watering cans and flowerpots decorated them rather than a lighterman pulling on a long, wooden tiller. Even some pleasure cruisers were appearing as the population became ever more affluent. All these pleasure craft needed somewhere to moor and be serviced so marinas were required and one of them was to be on possibly the finest winter roach section of the Navigation, between Stanstead Abbots and Rye

House, famous for the 'October Hole' a noted area for roach since before the Second World War.

The river had a slight flow, caused by the Magna Stream entering directly below the lock and, further downstream, a small tributary that we knew as the Piebald Stream entered on a bend in the river. It was the Piebald that was to be the marina and dredgers were cutting out the banks to widen and deepen it. Billy Allen had heard that the roach were 'going ballistic' in the coloured water so we decided to have a look. The first time we went it was crazy, with roach to well over a pound feeding heavily so we decided to share the news with some of the others and a 'club outing' was arranged, including Bob the Pipe and his mate, Bob the Dog (don't ask!).

We chose our swims, slightly upstream of the confluence seemed best but Graham Blake sat almost dead opposite, fishing through a well-worn gap in a large bed of bankside rushes. We caught a few fish, not as many as previously, but enough to make it a cracking day for all... except Blakey who had missed bite after bite. Bob the Pipe strolled down to see him and asked what was the matter.

"I don't believe it," said Blakey (Victor Meldrew could have been based on Blakey – indeed the Blakey character in the ancient *On the Buses* series had a similar approach to life, believing that misfortune was sent exclusively to him). "I'm getting a bite-a-chuck and can't hit 'em. I'm just laying on" (fishing over-depth with a float and holding the bait still on the bottom) "and it's going under every cast. I've only had a couple of little roach and dropped a couple" (had them slip the hook).

"Let's have a butchers," said Bob and knelt on one knee beside Graham, whose float looked like it was suffering from the tremors: dipping and bobbing before slipping under the surface. The resulting strike connected with fresh air and an exasperated cry escaped from Blakey's lips.

"Let 'em 'ave it a bit longer," said Bob and, sure enough next cast resulted in a similar bite which, to his credit, Graham left longer before striking, this time hooking a fish that bent the rod before, once again, coming off the hook. The float smashed down on the surface as Graham vented his anger on his tackle.

"Not long enough," said Bob. "Wait until I tell you."

On went a fresh maggot, in went the float and, a minute or so later, under went the float. Bob waited for a full 10 seconds before saying: "Right, just lift gently, don't strike, I reckon you're pulling the hook out." By now the rest of the group were gathered round, in the gloom of winter twilight, hoping for Graham to catch the big roach he so desperately wanted.

Following orders, he gingerly lifted the rod, which took on a satisfying curve as whatever was on the end offered fitful resistance before yielding to the pressure. As the 'fish' hit the surface, Bob let out a huge, single peal of laughter. It was a fish alright, a CRAYfish, its little pincers stuffing Blakey's maggots into its mouth, with the line tangled round a couple of legs.

Blakey went potty, calling Bob, the little crustacean and all and sundry every name he could lay his tongue to.

"You knew, didn't you," he snarled at Bob.

"I had a good idea, I've been watching them climb up the reeds, and your keepnet, for the last half-hour," came the reply. "I reckon there's loads of 'em down there, like in *The Perishers*, and as they saw you fishing there the Mighty Leader called out: 'Hallelujah Brothers: It's the Eyeballs in the Sky.'"

Those of you familiar with the *Daily Mirror* of the time will undoubtedly recall Maurice Dodd's wonderful comic strip, featuring characters such as Wellington, Maisie, Marlon and Baby Grumpling, plus Boot, an Old English

Sheepdog. Each year the comic strip took them on holiday, to the rockpool, where the inhabitants of the 'pooliverse' were gathered by their senior crab leader to observe the miracle of the 'Eyeballs in the Sky' as Boot stuck his nose into their world.

We all knew the cartoons and were rolling around on the floor, tears in our eyes, while Graham became angrier and angrier. He is a fine angler and has the ability to laugh at himself, but not on this particular occasion, when several others are doing it for him.

I related this story on my radio programme and Chris Gadsden, himself an angler and secretary of Uxbridge Rovers Angling Society, who is married to Maurice Dodd's daughter, Catherine, contacted me. I am now the EXTREMELY proud owner of TWO original Perishers' strips, drawn by Maurice Dodd, featuring this annual, mystical event. Chris and I have fished together a few times since, including when he and his lovely wife joined us in Key West, on our 'boy's trip' for a few days.

Around this time I was working in George's Tackle, in Mare Street, Hackney; a shop not short of characters in the customers ranks. One of them was 'Waggy' Parker who frequently travelled to Teddington Lock on the train, using his bicycle to ride to the station and from there to the river. He had the fortunate trait of not feeling the cold and would always show up at the shop in a tweed sports jacket, open-neck shirt and grey flannel trousers, usually on a Friday evening. He even participated in some night fishing in said attire, taking with him a minimum amount of tackle; just a single rod, tied to the crossbar of his bike, the rest of his kit in an army surplus khaki shoulder bag. His bait went in a bucket, also used to bring home any decent-sized eels, which were his favourite food: he jellied them himself.

One Saturday lunchtime, having spent the entire morning sieving, then selling maggots and casters, Waggy barged in through the front door of the shop:

"Here, what do you think of THIS," he said. "I was down the weir (Teddington Weir) last night, not caught a thing, when I had a right slow bite. I picked up the rod and struck but I thought I'd hooked a branch. I wound in and, sure enough, I could make out a bundle of twigs on me 'ook, from the lights on the swing bridge." (A suspension bridge crosses the weir stream that swings, rather disconcertingly, if enough people cross it at the same time.)

He continued: "I dragged it up the bank and it started walking away, so I got me bucket, stuck it over it and sat on it all night. I could hear and feel this bloody thing scrabbling about and was too scared to lift the bucket orf it. Any-old-how, when it gets light, I drags the bucket across the gravel, away from the water, and 'as a butchers. I thought to meself 'it's a bleedin coconut with legs'. It was only a crab, bloomin' great biggun too. I got the train to Richmond, the Tube to South Ken(sington) and took it to the Science Museum." (In fact he meant the Natural History Museum, almost next door). "They had a look at it and reckon it's a bleedin' Chinese mitten crab! Waddya think of that?"

I was, once again, crying with laughter: Waggy's description was so brilliant and enacted with such vigour and what's more I hadn't the slightest clue as to what was coming next during it.

The rest of the shop, customers, George and his wife Muzzy were enrapt by the story, eventually George asked what I found so funny.

"I've just imagined that crab, walking best part of 6000 miles from China, having a nice quiet snack then being dragged out of the Thames and having a bucket stuck over it."

A mitten crab gets its name from a furry covering on the pincers. It is not an attractive colour, indeed not to put too fine a point on it, they have the appearance of having been used for a purpose usually associated with toilet paper.

Nowadays mitten crabs are common from the Pool of London as far upstream as Walton. Eventually they will meet the 'Eyeballs in the Sky' as the equally invasive American signal crayfish, imported from the USA as a food source that have populated many rivers in the south of the country, destroying the native white-clawed crayfish population as they go, courtesy of a deadly fungal disease known as 'crayfish plague' to which the intruders are immune, travel downstream. Donald Judd, a contributor to my radio programme, composed this poem about a similar battle that may take place on the River Lea, also afflicted with signal crayfish upstream and mitten crabs in the lower reaches. I reproduce it with his permission:

The Battle of the River Lea

At the break of dawn, battle lines were drawn,
Upon the watery field,
The commanders of the armies met,
But neither one would yield.

So, angry crustaceans, from two mighty nations,
Drew their deadly claws,
The Chinese mittens and American signals,
Were to fight the mother of wars.

They would meet to fight, at Waltham, at night,

Keith Arthur

On the bed of the river Lea,

The commanding crab, ordered out loud,

"Forward, on the count of three."

But the signal crays, were so amazed,

When the crabs marched sideways instead,

"If that's their idea of going forward,

They're mad," their general said.

But they didn't expect, any hope of respect,

As an outflanking manoeuvre took place,

And before you say, a word such as 'knife',

They were staring them straight in the face.

Both generals had found, some higher ground,

At precisely seven of the clock,

And as each observed the battle develop,

The mittens hit a stumbling block.

Their second in command, said, "I'll be darned,

By God, there goes my claw,"

The mitten's general turned and replied,

"By God, sir, so I saw."

But those crafty crabs, lifted their dabs,

And in a pincer movement – pounced,

And turned upon the crayfish,

Fishing

Keith Arthur

Who were all unceremoniously trounced.

The Yankies were banished, and suddenly vanished,
From north of that battle zone,
And the Chinese crabs with their mitts on their dabs,
Now thrive there, by themselves, on their own.

Apparently the mitten crabs came here in ballast on Chinese freighters and once established in the river, marched inexorably westwards. There is one under almost every rock on the tidal river now and a sharp frost coinciding with a low tide seems to kill off any 'shedding'; their bodies being easily visible on the following low water.

Amazingly the VERY slightly brackish water at Teddington now sees bass, mullet and flounders as regular visitors, residents even – I landed my first Thames flounder from a swim close to the 'Thames Stone', which marks the end of the Port of London Authority and the start of the old Thames Conservancy. The stone is just a couple of hundred yards below Teddington Lock. That was in 1971 and it was over 13 inches long. They breed in the river upstream as far as this and a first light wading session sees tiny flounders fluttering away, escaping from being trodden on. When a huge sewage pollution struck the river, from good old Mogden Sewage Works at Isleworth, in 2005, the foreshore at Kew was paved with dead immature flounders.

During the 'draw-off' when the barrier which maintains a navigable depth between Richmond and Teddington locks is lifted for maintenance each year, allowing the river here to drop to the fullest extent of the tide, exposing yards of riverbed covered for the other 11 months of the year, I have a forage and, two years ago, on turning over a wooden crate, found inside five mitten crabs, which didn't surprise me to any great degree, but in with them was a dozen or so shrimps: not the small freshwater variety but *crangon crangon*, the brown shrimp! How they survive I don't know but their existence must have something to do with the massive growth in several tidal Thames fish, not least bream. A bream of 4 pounds was a monster 20 years ago, almost unheard of. Now the average size, by no means the biggest, is between 6 and 7 pounds.

But every time I see one of those crabs, I think of Waggy Parker, Bob the Pipe and the Eyeballs in the Sky.

Keith Arthur

Irish Adventures

In 1970, Efgeeco, (an acronym for FG, the owner's initials and co) the then-famous fishing tackle manufacturers, launched a revolutionary style of groundbait. Called 'Coax', the product came in a cardboard box and wasn't in the form of loose crumbs, as were all previous groundbaits, but was preformed into flat-topped, conical shapes, each one being maybe 2 inches in diameter at the base and slightly less than an inch at the top. A hole, half an inch in diameter, ran vertically through the centre. Also supplied was a device that fitted inside the hollow centre of the bait that, when threaded on the line, did away with swimfeeders. The cavity could alternatively be filled with maggots, plugged with a small amount of conventional groundbait at either end and thrown or catapulted into the swim. On first glance they looked exactly like the little cones of millet seed, with a bell on the bottom that my dad used to treat his budgerigars.

To launch the product, Efgeeco ran a competition: make a great catch using Coax and the nine finalists, one a month, will go to Ireland and fish a two-day match with a £500 prize fund, a considerable sum in 1970/71. My fishing pal Peter Burton had already qualified and as we were sharing our winnings at the time, he pushed me into having a stab. The obvious place was the lake by the Gaps and so it proved, a 172 pound bag of bream, caught using about a dozen packs of Coax, was sufficient for me to be invited.

Keith Arthur

We flew from Birmingham Airport, only my second flight having been to Brussels the year before to follow Arsenal in the Inter-Cities Fairs Cup final first leg, against Anderlecht. We had one small problem: back then good quality bait, maggots especially, were quite difficult to obtain in Ireland so Peter and I, plus three other anglers from our area, Fred Gladwin, John Carey and tackle shop owner George McCarthy, decided to take our own. Of course, being naive we simply turned up at the airport with 20 biscuit tins, lidless, filled with top-grade, perfectly fresh and quite smelly maggots. The baggage people didn't have a clue: they'd been slightly perturbed by our long rod bags – no special cases or the like were around then – and fishing baskets, now they had 20 tins of wriggly things to deal with. So, they called the captain! He came to meet us and was extraordinarily helpful. He told us that if we made carry-handles for the tins and covered them with sacking that wouldn't come off during the flight, our bait was welcome on Aer Lingus. Don't ask how we found sufficient hessian sacking but we did and our bait went on holiday!

Our party consisted of some truly magnificent anglers, including the legendary Ivan Marks and his Leicester Likely Lads team-mate Dave Downes. Alongside them was a great Somerset angler, Dave Searle, a Yorkshireman called Dave Taylor, the only non-match angler in the group plus us five southerners. Our host was Fred J Taylor, one of the finest specimen anglers of all time, then-*Angling Times* Floatmaker of the Year Peter Drennan, boss of the enormous Drennan International and still, to this very day, a personal friend. Photographer Alan Pond who would record the event for the angling press and Bill Knott (senior) completed the party but how he got there I have not the first clue! His son, Bill (junior) is now the leading angling bookmaker, a role started by his late father.

Keith Arthur

The 150 mile drive from Dublin to Belturbet in Co Cavan, where we stayed in the Seven Horseshoes Hotel, was brilliant. Anyone travelling to Ireland now would be pleased with the quality of the majority of roads: it wasn't so then, with no bypasses so most of the route went from countryside to village to countryside. We stopped for lunch in Navan, a name I knew because I was working in a furniture store at the time, specialising in carpet sales and Navan Carpets was a decent brand. I remember having steak, chips and fried onions, which seemed to be the usual garnish to steak, wherever we ate. The social atmosphere in the minibus following lunch was brilliant: the air quality less so! On arrival we checked in to the hotel, had dinner and crashed out, next day we would see the river and have a practice.

The Erne System has many flowing stretches where it is a true river and others where the Lough is so wide the opposite bank isn't visible. Belturbet sits on the river where it is a similar size to the Thames above Oxford with a good flow and, in those days, a super-abundance of fish, especially roach and bream. Practice went well and, although we weren't allowed on the match length, I could feel an affinity with the water. I fished opposite where peg 1 was to be, whilst most of the others either fished upstream in the more-productive area around the creamery, where the local area's milk was processed. It wasn't easy fishing where I sat but I had about 20 decent sized roach in my net when Fred J and Alan Pond strolled down, asking if I had any roach they could take as bait: they were off to catch some pike on the following morning. I offered them my net and they took maybe a dozen, knocking them on the head to use as deadbaits.

The following day was to be the first of the match and at breakfast – and if you've never had a *proper* Irish breakfast, I can tell you that lunch is unnecessary – everyone fancied downstream end peg, number 1, with peg

8 the probable no-hoper. I drew upstream end peg 9, a shallow swim, quite similar to some I'd fished on the Middle Thames with a steady flow about two rod lengths from the bank. Peg 1, the 'flyer' was occupied by Fred Gladwin, a Thames expert and a very good match angler but who could never be described as a 'speed merchant'.

At the end of the match Fred weighed in 37 pounds 9 ounces, mostly quality roach and a few skimmer bream for first place whilst I was back in sixth place with 33 pounds 5 ounces 8dr, made up of nearly 400 roach – I counted them – it was that close! Peter Burton and Ivan Marks were both in front of me too, so with two of the best match anglers of all time, to my mind, barring my way to the top of the board, I wasn't too confident.

The next day was a 'pleasure session' and we'd arranged to visit Killykeen on Lough Oughter. Hugh Gough, of the Inland Fisheries Trust, had told us where to go and even promised to leave bait in the swims – imagine that here! – and, true to his word, when we arrived there were boxes of Coax and a sack of breadcrumb waiting, in the best spots according to Hugh. It was then that the genius of Ivan really came to my attention because although his tackle basket looked like it had just survived the Great Fire of London, there were two bait boxes tucked in the corner, containing a sheep's heart in each which had been 'blown' by a special fly which produces a small, very soft maggot known in match angling as a 'gozzer'. One was natural, the other an orange colour, created by spreading annatto vegetable dye on it to produce a golden-coloured maggot.

We caught a load of bream, legering, and on our return to the Seven Horseshoes, Peter was convinced that we hadn't seen all of Ivan's tricks which, according to Ivan himself, he kept: "... up my pocket." We searched the backyard, the outbuildings and everywhere we could but found nothing.

Keith Arthur

Then Peter looked inside a cabinet, in the foyer, used for the hotel telephone and, lo and behold, inside was a pillowcase containing a gallon or so of pinkies! Peter only took about 25% of them!

The following day was the final part of the match, what we had gone there for and I was last in the queue to draw, taking the peg that was left – number 1!! I fished what I consider one of the best matches I ever did and despite the heckling of Bill Knott, won the day with 43 pounds 9 ounces of quality roach and one bream. I nearly fainted as I drew that solitary bream to the net as a huge pike attacked it, coming from beneath the reeds at my feet. Fred had lost a few roach to probably the same fish on day one.

My total, 74.14.8, was sufficient to win the £300 first prize, Peter fished a great match from horror-peg 8 to finish second, and £100, with Ivan in third place. I lost one of my £s to Peter Drennan who had challenged me to a match within a match. He fished the creamery peg and weighed 51 pounds so my real winnings were £299. As he said: "Lucky I didn't qualify myself and have to show you all how to do it." It was a great time.

Then we were called outside to witness something and there, on a trestle table in the hotel's backyard, lay a truly gigantic pike. Fred J had put my roach to good use AND invented a new style of pike fishing at the same time. The usual tactic with dead fish as bait was to attempt to make them look alive, usually by attaching a spinning vane or bending them using two hooks so they'd wobble. Fred tried wobbling – the baits that is – for a couple of hours with no success. Then he and Alan Pond, who was fishing with him, stopped for a cuppa so Fred simply let his deadbait sink to the bottom and left it there. Some while later, the rod started to bend and be dragged across the grassy bank. Fred picked it up, set the hooks and landed a monster pike of 32 pounds 2 ounces and that is what we were staring at. Legered deadbaiting was born!

Keith Arthur

I was at Peter Drennan's magnificent Oxford office recently and saw in the lobby a picture of Peter, Fred J and Alan, behind that trestle table, admiring Fred's pike. I may even have taken the picture myself. I hadn't seen it until that day!

The final part of the Belturbet saga took place that night as John Carey and I decided to try our luck at a local dance, held in a small town about 15 miles away that we'd been told about by a spectator at the match, who was to be a DJ there. We borrowed the minibus, found the place and arrived at about 9pm. He'd told us not to get there before 10.30pm but we disregarded him. The hall had maybe 10 people in it, all of school age, bopping away. I went to the bar to get us both a drink but it was soft drinks only – that's why it was best to turn up late; everyone else spent the best part of the evening getting juiced up in the pub!

We had a great time, the latter part of which remains in my memory – I'll simply say that the truism that there are: "… two certainties in life: death and a nurse" proved not far from fact. I hate to admit it, but my 'pulling gear', a dark-lilac coloured Prince of Wales check mohair suit, purple shirt and tie and purple chrome leather Chelsea boots, complete with Cuban heels (well, it was the early 1970s, come on) looked somewhat out of place amongst the local populace, but it worked. When we arrived back at the hotel, around 3am, we couldn't get in and spent the rest of the night in the back of that minibus.

I knew then that I'd be back and in fact there have been many happy returns, one of which came on what should have been my honeymoon. My wife and I were married on April 25th 1973 and on April 27th I was in Limerick, ready to fish for the LAA against Birmingham Angling Association on the 28th. We got beat – well, actually we got slaughtered – by Brum but in those days

Keith Arthur

their team contained 'imported' stars such as John Toulson (Notts Fed), Kevin Ashurst (Leigh) and Max Winters (Gloucester) who were at the very height of their powers. Add that on to Clive Smith, Ken Giles, Tony Rees, Lloyd Davies amongst others and it's understandable. I remember in the hotel bar the night following the match where we were given a celebratory dinner by the wonderful local people. I was talking to a man who wasn't into coarse fishing at all but lived for his salmon and sea trout on the Shannon. He was absolutely sloshed, so much so he couldn't open his eyes but that didn't stop him reaching into his inside suit jacket pocket and retrieving a fly box. He then systematically went through the contents, still with his eyes closed until, halfway through, he simply went to sleep.

Some of the team, who were also Terrapin members, returned to the hotel several times in the ensuing years and were always treated regally. They were often joined by other angling friends for the trip and there is a wonderful story that Tommy Young has told me several times.

One of the friends, Johnny Floyd, has a sleep problem: he can be sitting, in earnest conversation when, for no reason, he simply drops off. When he goes to bed at night he is almost impossible to wake, especially if he's had one or two – and several more – Guinness. One night he bid the group goodnight early, no later than 10pm and Tommy hatched a plan. A couple of hours later he requested a key for John's room and a group of them went in and carried Floydy, bed and all, into the car park. Once they parked his bed they retired for the night. John was woken the next morning by a motorist who needed his space!

Not all my memories of Ireland are as good: I was in Enniskillen in Northern Ireland when the IRA bombed the car park at the Sealink Angling Festival, in fact I was no more than 20 yards from the bomb when it exploded,

The best excuse for loafing in the countryside 153

killing three members of the British Army who had fished the event.

The year before, I had fished the Erne Baits Festival, along with my pals Pete Ottewill, Fred Brown, Lennie Goodwin and John 'Lasher' Larraman. Pete loved Northern Ireland – he was unfortunately struck down by cancer and died a couple of years ago but his memory lives on with a trophy named after him, fished for each year at Inniscarra Reservoir. Our home for the week was Lodge 12 outside the Killyhevlin Hotel, at the time the only one with a landing stage so we could fish for a couple of hours after the match. Oh yes, we were as keen as that! We all caught loads of fish; my total weight for five days of match fishing, just five hours a day, was a shade under 200 kilos, 440 pounds or well over 80 pounds a day!

One of the funniest memories involves Fred and Len. We had decided to eat Chinese for dinner and in Enniskillen there is a superb Chinese restaurant called the Silver Lough that also does carry-outs. We chose our meals, ordered everything we wanted, plus plenty of rice. Len was a stickler for cleanliness and when Fred took a bath, Len insisted that every minute remnant of personal existence was cleaned out. His favourite expression was: "I don't want to find a watch spring (piece of body hair) in there."

When we returned with the meal, Fred was still cleaning so we opened the bags to find what seemed an unusually large amount of boxes. We had ordered a portion of rice for every dish but unknown to us rice was included anyway. Len took all the excess rice, 5 boxes, and stacked it on a plate; it looked like a white version of the Devil's Tower in *Close Encounters of the Third Kind.* He then took a single spare rib and stuck it firmly on the summit of the mountain, placing it in our cabin's oven.

By the time Fred had scrubbed the bath to Len's satisfaction, we were all eating our meals. "Where's mine?" asked Fred.

Keith Arthur

"What did you order, a 27 with rice wasn't it?" said Len. "It's in the oven."

Fred's face was a picture but we gave him his real meal – we're good like that.

Finally, I returned to the scene of the Sealink bomb four years later to appear in my first angling videos, with Mark Downes, England international, starring in two of his own. I could possibly write a book about the 10 days but, don't worry anyone who was there, I won't. Again we stayed at the Killyhevlin, this time in the hotel proper – that's what a filming budget can do. We had a mixed crew: a couple of cameramen, Brian and Bill, a sound engineer and a photographer, Keith Juriansz. David Hall was director and Micky Shepherd, producer. Keith the photographer was on the naive side and took everything at face value, with no recognition of irony. He had a Peruvian father and had inherited his South American skin tone. On our final evening there David got him totally paralytic drunk, instructing the bar staff to add a double vodka to everything he ordered. When we sat down to eat he was rolling about in his chair. Micky, in the meantime, had somehow acquired a powerful water pistol and took to firing it so Keith was sprayed. He then aimed it at the ceiling above Keith's head and water was soon dripping down on to the table and his dinner.

With no more ado, Keith flew to the front desk and told the duty manager there may be a problem in a bedroom upstairs as water was leaking through the ceiling. He returned with the *owner* of the hotel, who looked at the damp patch, smiled and said:

"Now we have a honeymoon couple in that room. Maybe they've run a bath and something else has got in their minds." And with that he marched off to the stairs. Of course he found out the truth when he came back but it might have been as good a honeymoon as mine after that escapade.

One final story about Keith and David. Earlier in the week we had been having a general discussion about England's traffic problems when David said to Keith:

"What's it like where you come from? I know you don't drive, so how do you get around?"

Keith responded: "Oh, it's excellent. There are bus stops almost at the end of every road, we've got a great rail service and I can get almost anywhere in the country very easily."

"Wow that's great," said David. What part of Peru is that?"

"Oh, I wasn't talking about Peru. I come from Croydon…"

Keith Arthur

On the Fly

I had never even picked up a fly rod in anger until 1992 although I felt
qualified to talk about them when taking orders from my customers. By
this time I was working as a sales representative for Daiwa Sports, the UK
manufacturing and sales arm of Daiwa Seiko, Japan; the largest fishing tackle
manufacturers in the world. I had learned during my years in the retail
tackle trade of the requirements of a fly angler when buying a rod: the line
ratings, based on a scale developed by the Association of Fishing Tackle
Manufacturers of America, AFTMA for short, were designed as a means of
matching rods, reels and lines into compatible groups. That knowledge,
combined with a decent grasp of what is meant in rod design by 'tip action',
'through action' and some of the mechanics of casting, meant that I could BS
my way along. I still felt that I really should have a go but as an angler who
had made instructional-type videos on coarse fishing and who wrote regularly
in magazines, I was slightly reluctant to offer myself up to a professional
coach.

I was saved by a customer. Rick Nunn from the Tackle Up shop in Bury
St Edmunds in Suffolk is a brilliant fly angler who, along with his daughters
Rachael and Emma, both equally adept at what I thought was a potential
egg-on-face moment, organised three events each season for his customers at
Rutland Water, the 3000+ acre reservoir in England's smallest county. Indeed

Rutland is SO small it disappeared for a few years – almost like the lost city of Atlantis it seemed to be swallowed by the lake as it flooded! On one visit, it must have been a weak moment when Rachael and Emma were eating a jam doughnut each from the 10 pack I always took with me; Rick persuaded me I should join them on the next sortie. He would lend me all the necessary tackle, all I had to do was show up. Well, it would be fishing from a boat so it's unlikely I'd hook anything worse than myself. On the doughnut front, Emma had the unfortunate habit of biting into the back of the cake, opposite to the hole where the jam goes in, and often ended up wearing more jam than she ate.

To make sure I didn't appear a complete clown, I asked another customer to help me with casting. When anyone who has never fly-fished acts out a cast, they hold the arm still and flick the wrist back and forth. That is, I was soon to learn, precisely what NOT to do; in fact the man I asked, John Rolfe, told me that one tip he often gave was to tuck the end of the rod up a sleeve to keep the wrist as rigid as possible, just 'break' it at the final second. Rolfey, who I knew from his days as Lord and Master of the River Trent, where he was famous for pioneering waggler fishing, was running the fly fishing section at Walkers of Trowell, near Nottingham, and was an expert at Rutland, along with another former Trentman and idol of many anglers, John Dean. They caught trout as readily as they had roach on the great river when it was at its heyday during the 1970s and 80s. Rolfey used to say that if he was short of cash, all he'd do was get his match kit out and fish a Thursday Open at Burton Joyce. "Easier to win money there than it is to draw it from a cashpoint," he told me several times and he was only half-joking. I respected John because on my first visit to his favourite section at Burton Joyce, I drew peg 126 and he 'put me right', well right enough for me to finish fifth in a very high-class field with

Keith Arthur

14 pounds 14 ounces of fish on, yes you've guessed, the waggler.

John took me out the back of the shop where they had a casting pool; a strip of water maybe 20 yards long. He corrected my grip on the rod and got me into the timing of 'forward-1-2, back-1-2' allowing the rod to 'load', or compress, and act as a spring to throw the line forward. It stood me in fine stead until Charles Jardine, one of *the* great casters, got me to add a 'tap' at the top of the forward cast. He described it as the action of tapping a nail with a hammer. By the time we got to the day, I could at least not look like a total beginner.

As the boats at Rutland demand two anglers, I was paired with Graham Barry, the manager at the time of Marks and Marlow (my pal Roy and Ivan's shop) in Leicester. Graham is another brilliant all-round angler and we had a decent-enough day. He told me to use a black lure called an Ace of Spades to start and I caught my first fly-tempted rainbow trout within the first hour. It must have been starving because the rocking of the boat whilst casting caused havoc with my timing. But I, like that rainbow, was hooked and I have fly fished regularly since.

Once I had been contracted as the 'resident expert' on *Tight Lines*, invitations started arriving, one of which was to 'Press Day' at Hanningfield Reservoir near Chelmsford in Essex. I was excited as soon as I sat down in the lovely restaurant there for breakfast because, just a couple of seats away, was David 'Safe Hands' Seaman, still in his pomp for England and, more important still, Arsenal. What's more he knew me, having watched the show! We even managed to have him as a guest twice: once official, once less so. The official one was when I fished with David at Croxley Hall in Rickmansworth, now an exclusive carp syndicate but then a lovely fly-only trout water. The second was when the draw for the 1998 World Cup had taken place and he was a guest on *Sky Sports Centre* (now News), along with Colin Calderwood, Spurs centre-back. It was the night of the 150th *Tight Lines* and the producer, Andy Storey, had invited the show's two previous producers along as guests to a 'bit of a do' afterwards, along with other crucial members of the teams since the programme's inception. Bruno Brookes was the presenter at the time and we had a guest each show. As David left the News studio, series one producer Darren Williams cheekily nabbed him and said: *"Tight Lines* is on in there, it's the 150th show. Fancy going on?" So, during the next commercial break, in came the great man. We didn't even have time to find him a chair so he crouched on his haunches for 15 minutes until the show ended. Back to the fishing and Hanningfield…

On my first visit I was paired with Charles Jardine and thought it would be a perfect time to have my distinctly shabby technique somewhat refined. What I hadn't expected was that the temperature would be dropping like a stone all day – and it started very cold, with frost about and ice on any puddles. I asked Charles what lures we should tie on but he insisted that they'd be eating buzzers, which are imitations of chironomid larvae that rise to the surface to hatch into midges, a tiny air-bubble helping the rise, duplicated on the imitation either by a tiny bead or a white 'moustache'. I couldn't see many 'coming off' as the technical term goes, especially as, when retrieving my fly line to put 'life' into the fly, I was peeling a layer of ice off it! The best part of the day, barring breakfast, was lunch and the third best bit was going home! But I did get that 'tapping a nail' casting tip.

I was invited back again the following year, this time being partnered in the boat by Mick Toomer. Mick was known as a genuine expert big-fish angler, especially for pike, but his angling had taken a bit of a back seat as he was developing some fisheries for his local council at Basildon in Essex. I wasn't

Keith Arthur

aware that he fly fished but he did, and very well too. Like many of the true greats, Mick was concerned about catching fish above all else and whereas I was quite happy to catch a couple of nice rainbow trout to take home, Mick's competitive instinct had kicked in and he'd found they wanted something big and orange, so he gave it to them. I plodded away, casting and slowly retrieving, whilst Mick whacked it out as far as he could and ripped it back, using the aggressive nature of the quarry to snap at his rapidly-retreating lure.

We were fishing at anchor and the boat was swinging in the gentle breeze, causing Mick to slightly shut my casting window, forcing me to cast to my left – he was sitting on my right in the boat. By now I was using something big and orange too: a lure known as a tadpole which boasts a lead shot at the front of the hook to give it weight to sink and be retrieved well beneath the surface. Something had to give and it did: with a dull thud, on the forward cast, my fly stuck in the middle of Mick's scalp, where his hair was at its thinnest. (Too polite: his bald patch.) I eased it out, and Mick took it in good part. Twenty minutes later I did it again, this time it was a touch more serious and the hook needed more persuasion to come free. I apologised greatly and suffered plenty of ribbing when we pulled in for lunch.

By some fluke I drew Mick as partner again a year later and, as the names were announced, he pulled from his bag a Second World War firewarden's helmet, as worn by Bill Pertwee in *Dad's Army* on BBC television. He fished in it too! A lovely touch by a genuinely nice man that made everyone laugh and put me at ease. I stuck to the lighter, less dangerous buzzers.

The greatest joy I obtain from fly fishing is that it allows me to be more of a purist than I am when coarse fishing. I suppose because I came into it late I can appreciate it for what it is and actually obtain great pleasure from simply casting well. Catching fish isn't as essential as it is when I am bait fishing,

The best excuse for loafing in the countryside

2161

which is just as well really, especially when salmon fishing with a fly, a pursuit I have tried three times for three days at a stretch.

My pals Billy Allen and Brian Gent both gave up coarse fishing some years ago to concentrate on their fly fishing and then took it one stage further and fished almost exclusively for salmon. Mind you, I use the term 'salmon fishing' very loosely indeed: it is more like salmon waiting, salmon avoiding or the like. On the three occasions I have spent holidays with my two mates, on Scotland's River Nith, I have remained a salmon-free zone. Brian books the beats (sections of salmon fisheries are called 'beats', probably because that's what you want to do to yourself at the end of the day) and we collect him from his Cumbrian home on route north.

We have twice fished on the Duke of Buccleuch's estate, close to the magnificent Drumlanrig Castle. I have sat by the fishing hut, eating my packed lunch, watching a dipper work the tiny stream that bypasses the stone weir there. I have stopped on the drive down to the river to watch a buzzard dismembering the morning's catch, sitting on a tree stump no more than 10 feet from my car. I have even seen a couple of salmon, one each to Bill and Brian but they were not the 'bars of silver' usually associated with the species, but very red, cock fish that had been in the river for months and were preparing for what normally turns out to be their last action: procreation. It's not as much fun as the prenuptial cigarette I once enjoyed (I quit smoking in 1986, after 25 years of burning money), at least as far as the salmon is concerned.

Our third trip was to a section known as Friars Carse, managed by the hotel of that name. It *looks* an excellent beat with several features that possibly could hold salmon if the river wasn't too high, too low, too clear, too coloured, too warm or too cold. All it can't be is too wet! I at least caught a fish there when, whilst allowing a lure (the river was 'wrong' for fly fishing; as wrong as it was for having salmon in attendance) known rather appealingly as the Flying Condom, or Flying C in either mixed company or Ireland, to swing around in the current. Suddenly it stopped and, miracle of miracles, I remembered what to do should a fish happen along, and NOT strike. I tightened the line, as I'd been instructed and waited for the fish to bolt downstream, setting the hook and, maybe, threatening my continence. It happened, very meekly, but there was definitely a fish on my hook, it was swirling on the surface.

I wound it in and was disappointed to see it was a grayling. What I didn't notice at the time was that it was a HUGE grayling, well over 2 pounds, possibly even 3 pounds and that is an absolute monster. But it wasn't a salmon and, to date, nor has any other fish that I have hooked been. However, I have caught a tuna on fly, and not too many anglers can say that.

Although I have designated a chapter for Key West tales, this is a genuine fly fishing story so it fits here well. On our annual pilgrimage we had booked some days fishing with Capt Manny Ravelo on his light tackle boat, *Another Grouper*, named for his favourite species. Manny loves fishing the Gulf of Mexico waters; the shallow wrecks, usually in 60-90 feet of water, target-towers built there by the US Air Force and shrimp boats seeking the famous Key West pink shrimp, all provide great habitat and feeding for many species. Unfortunately the price of fuel has seen both the numbers of shrimp boats and the number of captains prepared to make the trip, drop. It can be a 70-mile one-way ride now to find a shrimper and even then it might be a 'nobody's home' on the big fish score.

This day happened before the massive increase in fuel prices and just 30 miles out we started to find the odd shrimp boat. These trawlers fish all night, when the shrimp rise in the water, clean their catch at first light, then rest up all day before repeating as before. The bycatch rate is very high but it is mostly small, non-edible-to-humans fish that get caught in the trawl and are either dumped back to sea, dead, not that bad a thing as it is recycled into edible fish in most cases, or bagged and frozen and sold to the Key West light tackle boats as chum (bait). That being said, some species, red snapper especially, have declined and the shrimpers carry the can.

The first shrimp boat we found showed plenty of fish on our fish finder so Manny threw in a couple of handfuls of chum, collected on a previous trip to the Gulf, but nothing came up to eat it. Another boat was visible on the horizon so we motored over to it. These light tackle boats can travel at speeds in excess of 50mph and often cruise at 35-40mph, so journeys are nowhere near as long as they would be on an average UK charter boat. On reaching it Manny tossed in some more chum and on the second handful a bunch of bonito, which look like half-mackerel, half-tuna weighing in between 6 and 15 pounds, came up and ate it. He repeated the process and more joined in. He was staring intently at the water because although they are superb sport and one of the toughest fighters in the oceans, bonito aren't considered to be game fish: tuna are and he wanted to see the darker, thicker shape of a blackfin tuna. Although one of the smallest members of the tuna clan, blackfin are every bit as good fun – in fact a 20 pound blackfin is more fun than a 500 pound bluefin, although I'd settle for the back-breaking fight those leviathans offer. What I *really, really* want is a yellowfin tuna of more than 150 pounds but that will have to wait, because this is a blackfin story.

On the third handful of feed a couple of blackfin joined the hundred or so bonito flashing for the dead fish Manny was throwing. He cut a small majorra (similar to one of our black sea bream but maximum size 10 inches or so) into five pieces and tossed that. Even more blackfins appeared. By now we had drifted 50 or 60 yards from the boat but the fish had come with us. More small amounts of chum were thrown, more blackfins, less bonito showed up. I learned how to chum blackfin from Capt Manny that day and I am forever grateful. By the time we were a hundred yards from the shrimp boat Manny decreed it was time to catch a tuna and hooks baited with chunks of chum were thrown in. Tommy Young hooked up, Ross Nursey hooked up and I hooked up. We boated two of the three. Even catching tunas the size of the average blackfin, 15 pounds or so, is a demanding task and I wanted one on fly before I became too tired – or too old come to that! Jason Lowe, an incredibly gifted fly angler and fly tyer had created some patterns for me to try, using large hooks wrapped with plenty of tinsel. Manny told me to drop the fly in and throw one morsel of chum close to it. I did so and an ultra-aggressive tuna beat the few remaining bonito to the fly, while a bonito grabbed the free lunch.

The fly line melted from the reel, closely followed by a couple of hundred yards of backing as the fish tried to make it back to the sanctuary of the shrimp boat. I could see the bright yellow fly line describing a massive arc in the water as the tuna swam first left, then right, against the drag. Rather worryingly, beneath the boat I could see three BIG sharks, attracted by the action, one of them already having bitten a tuna being played in half. I didn't want to lose my prize to a lemon shark at any cost.

After maybe 10 or 15 minutes my tuna came within sight – only there were two! 'My' fish was being followed by another, slightly smaller specimen. In the crystal-clear water I could see them, maybe 30-40 feet down, circling as tuna do against the resistance of the line. The sharks meantime were being teased away by Manny, with a half bonito on a rope.

Eventually I could see what had happened: one of the tuna we'd hooked and lost when it broke the line had tangled with my leader, the length of fluorocarbon line used to connect the main fly line to the hook. The fish actually *on* my hook looked enormous, bigger than any blackfin I'd ever encountered previously. Luckily, shortly afterwards the line untangled and it was me versus one, rather than two, tuna. Once the fish was on the surface Manny reached over and grasped it by the narrow wrist of the tail and swung it aboard. We took its picture and put it in the ice box for dinner. On arriving back at the dock we weighed the fish on the officially registered scales at 30 pounds and it was 10 months later that I discovered that, when I'd caught it, it would have been a world record on 20 pound leader, which is what I used. Even now it equals the record. I hope one day we can get out into the Gulf of Mexico and find some more blackfin. I have caught them on bait but fly fishing for them is something else and if good old Rick Nunn hadn't convinced me, I would never have known it.

Keith Arthur

Paradise Found

During the five years I spent working for Daiwa Sports, my then-colleague
Roy Marlow was constantly relating stories of big fish in warm oceans. He
had been on the first ever ABU Dream Trip, awarded by the Swedish tackle
company to people who caught special fish using their tackle. The first of
those trips was to the Florida Keys and although he subsequently went to
many other exotic destinations, it was The Keys that became his regular, well,
if not obsession then something pretty close. I was tempted – who wouldn't
be – but it sounded an awful lot of money for a couple of weeks fishing.
However, as in many things in life, it needs what appears to be a miracle at
the time to make wishes come true.

Daiwa was in the ascendancy as far as the UK fishing tackle market was
concerned, even during the downturn in the economy of the early 1990s –
another one fuelled by house-price speculation! At the annual sales meeting
in October 1990, we, members of the sales team and Roy, who was our
senior consultant, were told that if we achieved our budget we would have
a 'special' sales meeting next time. If we beat it by 10% or more, that special
meeting would be somewhere even more special. I think Roy had arranged
this, in cahoots with sales director John Middleton and although I didn't dare
believe it, my 'best guess' was the special place would be The Keys.

Despite the gloom many in the tackle trade were suffering, a good sales team and a great product range saw us beat our budget by 11%! We were going somewhere special and at the October meeting in 1991 we were told that, in February 1992, we would be going to The Keys for five days: three days would be work and two wouldn't, we'd be going fishing. That proved inspirational and our annual run of trade shows flew by with great orders being taken – everyone was a winner!

I had never flown transatlantic before, the furthest I had travelled was to Portugal: the Miami flight is four times longer but I don't remember falling asleep on the flight – or for the few days before it come to that. I had premature jet lag! Robin Morley, who was part of the team and is the current sales and marketing director at Daiwa Sports, sat next to me and, in those days, he didn't mind a drop of lager, so much so that the cabin staff said: "Look, it's there in the fridge, in the corner of the galley. Just help yourself."

The impact of stepping from the air conditioned coolness of Miami Airport into the humidity and noise of the outdoors for the first time is amazing. The arrivals area is beneath departures, in what appears to be a huge tunnel and the roar of diesel motors on the multitude of courtesy buses, enhanced by the thrumming of every vehicle's air con unit, literally takes the breath away. Once in our rental 'minivan' in USA terms, minibus to us, we were on the way to The Keys, a journey that I have undertaken many times since, on very different roads as the improvements have been massive, and each time I think I have smiled for the entire journey.

If you have never been to Florida, it is very far from being all-Disney, as many people think. In fact I don't think I've ever seen those flat, black ears there. The land is as flat as a pancake. For the area around Miami and the Florida Everglades, imagine our fens only hotter, and spreading for thousands of square miles and you'd be close. The highest point above sea-level in the entire state is 345 feet but the highest point in The Keys – with one manmade exception – is on Lignumvitae Key, close to the US1 road near the Village of Islands, Islamorada. It stands proudly 18 feet above the waves. We were to be staying at Marathon, 110 miles south-west of Miami, 45 miles from the end of the Keys chain of islands, Key West. Roy had found us a couple of very high-class condos in Faro Blanco Marina, where the marina scenes in *True Lies* were filmed.

The sales meetings were probably excellent but I don't remember a thing about them; it is difficult for me to forget one single second of the fishing. My first day out was with Capt Butch Hewlett, aka The Mullet Man. This had nothing to do with his tonsorial proclivity and all to do with his day job: catching mullet to sell as anglers' bait. Mullet are one of the prime baits used in the middle and lower Keys for tarpon, in the season from May to September when the Silver Kings shoal by the many bridges that carry the road south from Miami. They also work well for sharks and it is astonishing to sit within 50 feet of the main highway fighting a bull or lemon shark weighing over 200 pounds. It is not unusual to encounter a giant hammerhead either – but more of that later.

Butch ran an 'offshore' boat then, possibly a 31-footer, with an enclosed air-conditioned cabin and flying bridge, from which he drove the vessel. The back fishing area comfortably accommodated the three of us using it: me, sales director John and colleague Dave Roberts. We were bottom fishing with pieces of fish – 'cut bait' as the locals know it – and had put together a decent catch of mangrove snapper, small grouper and Spanish mackerel which are not unlike our mackerel but with mean teeth. Butch had also drifted a small livebait out the back, under a float, to attract something larger, with the rod placed in a holder.

Keith Arthur

The biggest thrill of my day was when I hooked a fish that seriously did NOT want to come and join us in the boat. It dived for the bottom and made some powerful, surging runs. I had never previously experienced a fight like it: the speed and strength of the fish in such warm water was unbelievable, especially when, at last, I brought it to the surface. It was a new species for me too, a cobia, maybe 12 or 15 pounds in weight and too SMALL to keep! The minimum size is 38 inches for a 'keeper' and this was a few inches shy, so we took its picture and returned it alive and still very much kicking!

We three were concentrating on our bottom fishing, catching fish regularly. John had placed himself next to the livebait rod and when he heard the reel screech as line was dragged from it, he automatically dropped his own rod into a holder and grabbed the other, which was bucking and bending to an alarming angle. Dave and I stopped fishing and turned to watch, with Dave looking back to see if we could find a clue as to what had been hooked – it didn't take long! Maybe 30 yards behind the boat a large, angry pelican was sticking its head under water, filling its bill to prevent being 'landed' by a big Yorkshireman. Dave had picked up John's video camera, on instruction given before we knew it was a bird rather than fish, and was filming the entire story for posterity. Dave is an avid photographer and has a huge collection of prints going back to black-and-white days of angling exploits so he was used to a camera... stills camera that is. He was wielding the video recorder like a box brownie, changing at will from 'portrait' to 'landscape' mode so, when watching the tape afterwards, it appeared that the pelican was making steep, banking manoeuvres, somehow dragging the Gulf of Mexico with it!

Although we performed a perfect 'catch and release' on the pelican we had enough fish in our ice box to take back for dinner, the excellent Kelsey's

Keith Arthur

Restaurant at the resort cooking our catch, as many Florida Keys restaurants still do.

Whilst at dinner that night two couples, one with a young child, were sitting at a table close by. They heard our accents and one of the men came over, asking if we would like to join them in a celebratory drink, as he had just driven to victory in the Daytona 500 and was staying at Faro Blanco. Knowing nothing of NASCAR at the time, but having heard of the race and knowing its importance, we felt honoured. Davey Allison, who we later found out to be the man concerned, was tragically killed in a helicopter crash in 1993.

The next day was work – sort of – then on to our second day's fishing. This time I was drawn to partner Robin Morley in Capt Mike Hewlett's skiff. These boats are designed to fish the extreme shallow water flats around Florida Bay and the nearshore Atlantic Ocean, which is reached by simply crossing to the opposite side of the road! Most skiffs can operate in well under 12 inches of water and can run at full speed – and that can be 50mph+ – in 2 feet. The captain, or guide, as flats boat captains are more commonly known, have a vast knowledge of the huge areas of shallow water in the region: in the entire expanse of Florida Bay the average depth is 4 feet, and mostly less than 2 feet. In these food-rich warm shallows cruise various species, according to the time of year. Bonefish, tarpon and permit are the three 'big game' species. Bonefish are resident most of the year and swim in small age-group shoals, the older and bigger the fish, the smaller the shoal. Sometimes really huge bonefish will be loners or, more usually, pairs. They are virtually see-through and can be easier spotted either when their silver sides flash in the sun or when they upend to feed in very shallow water and their tails pierce the surface. My motto for spotting bonefish is as follows: "If you can see a bonefish, it's a bonnethead shark; if you *think* you can see a bonefish, it's a barracuda but if the guide tells you there's a bonefish and you can't see it, he's right!"

When working the flats the guides raise a small platform on the stern of the skiff and using a long pole, nowadays carbon fibre, they propel the boat by pushing whilst balancing on the platform. Some of the guides are pretty large units – Capt Mike being one of them – yet their agility and balance never ceases to amaze.

Tarpon are slightly easier to spot, possibly because the average Silver King on the flats will be 4-6 feet long and 40-100 pounds in weight. Bonefish are very similar to barbel in both shape and size so much smaller targets. Tarpon are the largest of the herring family and have the disarming ability to breathe air so when the angler feels he's taking charge as the fish rolls and gasps in a lungful, what is really happening is the fish is rebuilding his energy cells. When hooked, tarpon will leap in the air, often 6-8 feet clear of the water, shaking their heads. The gills rattle and flare and the angler must 'bow to the King', lowering the rod and slackening the line to prevent a snap-off.

Permit are possibly the most prestigious prize on the flats. Members of the jack family, these beautiful, flat-bodied fish, similar shaped to our bream, cruise around searching for swimming crabs and shrimps. They are as spooky as hell and fight as hard, when hooked, as any fish I have ever encountered. A 15 pound permit will often strip 200 yards of line in the first run and make a few more runs too. Out of the water they look like they have backs made of pewter with chromed sides and golden patches close to the anal fin and tail. The sickle tail is often the giveaway to the guide as it breaks surface when the fish are in extremely shallow water.

It is often the case that only a few fish are spotted on a flats trip and casts have to be 100% accurate, landing the bait or lure precisely where the guide indicates. He gives his instructions using a clock-face grid, with the bow of the boat being 12. The distance from the boat is barked out in feet, so "10 o'clock, 30 feet" means slightly to the left of the bow.

Robin's rod was armed with a plug lure, hoping to spot an early-season tarpon or one of the smaller, resident fish that stay all winter around the mangroves, whereas mine was baited with a crab; ideal for permit or bonefish and unlikely to be ignored by a tarpon either. Mike had been poling for a long time on a very difficult, flat-calm, sunny day: perfect for a tan, disaster for seeing fish and being able to approach them as the sun reflects from the flats surface of the water. A slight ripple, diffusing our image and breaking up the reflection is perfect – or so I'm told: in 15 years I don't recall seeing it!

Then, from the cover of a stand of mangroves, a permit appeared. It was in maybe 2 feet of water and seemed to fill it, being fully 30 pounds and obviously hunting grub. Mike whispered as loud as he dared: "Permit, 10 o'clock going right, 25 feet. Put that crab 5 feet in front of his nose."

With shaking hands, I cast as accurately as I could, maybe slightly too close but the fish didn't spook, it merely turned and started to swim towards my crab. Time stood still – as time often does in similar situations – but it stood still long enough for Robin to throw his plug at the fish, nearly hitting it on the head! It didn't take kindly to that and, without any appreciable rush, waddled back to the mangroves from whence it came.

Capt Mike went absolutely ballistic! "Who told you to cast that goddam lure?" is about the only repeatable thing he screamed at Robin. We were to return fishless.

I had the great pleasure to fish with Capt Mike some years later, when he took me from Marathon, via the 'back-country highway' – across Florida Bay – in his skiff to fish the area I now know as 'Pearl Basin', to the north-east of Key West. He set the boat to drift along a channel, where 3 feet of water dropped into 8 feet. I was using a new reel, of which I was quite proud as it was a brand new model. I had shown Mike who seemed slightly less impressed; most of the guides prefer their anglers to use the tackle they provide as they can be sure of its effectiveness. I was even using my own rod, a 10 foot model designed for salmon spinning.

I had already captured a blacktip shark of 30 pounds or so, the blacktip being one of the few shark species that will take an artificial lure. I then hooked a tarpon of maybe 40 pounds, my first on a lure. It jumped, rolled and put in some enormous runs but with Capt Mike's help and expertise of keeping me in touch with the fish by allowing the boat to be towed by it, I eventually had the fish lying alongside the boat. Mike reached down with his 'hook-out' tool and released it. I was absolutely chuffed to bits as although I had caught bigger tarpon on bait, that was my first on an artificial lure. I took off my shirt to splash some seawater on my sweaty torso just as Capt Mike throttled up to return to the top of the drift. It was the last time I ever saw that t-shirt as it blew over the side of the skiff and disappeared backwards at 45mph. Luckily Mike had some powerful sunscreen and I smothered myself in it!

Next drift I hooked and released an even bigger tarpon, a fish Capt Mike estimated at 110 pounds and, looking at the photos right now, I still can't argue.

Next drift I nearly fell from my precarious perch as a MASSIVE tarpon swirled at the plug as I lifted it out at the end of the retrieve. Lesson learned; always give the lure a few side-to-side pulls beside the boat, with 8 feet or so of line out. It can pay dividends.

The reel had performed very well and even Mike was beginning to be impressed when out of the blue, a monster snatched my lure. Roy Marlow was following in a skiff operated by Capt Tom Kokenge, one of the premier permit guides of the Lower Keys, and even he stopped as a 7 foot-plus tarpon launched itself from the water, gill-plates rattling as it attempted to throw Capt Mike's Creek Chub Pikey lure. I have caught and released tarpon estimated at 180 pounds and this was every bit as big, possibly bigger. It leapt again, I bowed again and it set off on a long run towards what we call Demolition Key, where munitions are dumped after testing by the nearby naval base. Capt Mike looked at me, smiled and said: "How much line does that fancy goddam reel hold?" "450 yards," I replied. "Well, I hope it's enough," he said. I was beginning to get worried!

Maybe 20 minutes, and two more huge jumps later, my tarpon took to the skies again, only this time it threw the lure back at me, treble hooks being notoriously difficult to stick in to their extremely bony jaws.

Roy and Capt Tom had followed the battle for the mile or so it had been fought over, Roy wanting some pictures of this fish-of-a-lifetime. He didn't get them and I didn't get the fish but I don't need photos to remind me, I promise you that!

The next time that 'goddam reel' had as severe a test was on a day out from Key West with the legendary Capt Jack Kelly on his old boat, *Windy Day*. He now has a glorious new version, a 29 foot SeaVee, with two 225hp outboards on the back. His old boat had similar power but was a slightly less stable but, as we proved, unsinkable, Mako model. Jack is probably the finest tarpon guide fishing from Key West, the harbour being his second home from late February, when the first migratory schools use the harbour as a highway from the Gulf of Mexico to the flats beyond, until June when he trailers his boat to mid-Florida to ride out the extreme heat, humidity and hurricanes of summertime Key West. Now in his 70s, Jack is still 'The Man'.

On the same trip was Roy Marlow and our old pal, tackle dealer Jack Simpson. Jack has fished with Roy on the Keys and many other dream destinations and although on occasion they fight like cat and dog, they are wonderful company and truly fabulous anglers in all branches of the sport. They are also kings of wind-up! We had motored beyond the reef to the west of Key West in search of sailfish on the edge of the Gulf Stream. It was another hot, virtually windless day and not much was happening. The boat was free-drifting and we had four rods, each with a Styrofoam 'bobber' (float to us!) supporting a threadfin herring livebait. Suddenly, with an almost audible 'plop' Roy's float went down. He picked up the rod and the float bobbed back up. Ten seconds later Jack Simpson's did the same trick. "Get ready Keith," said Roy: "There's probably a small pod of sailfish cruising by. They've nicked our baits and yours will be next."

Sure enough, a few seconds later my float submerged violently and line started to pour from my 'goddam reel'. Roy shouted "Don't strike yet. Count seven then whack it." I got to six and a half, closed the bail arm and, well, whacked it, the rod taking an alarming curve as the fish, which was patently less happy with the outcome than I, departed towards Cuba, rather rapidly.

"Definitely a sail, ain't it Jack," said Roy in his Leicester accent. Simpson nodded and Kelly shook his head, something I have witnessed many times. Line was simply melting from the reel so I tightened the drag, the only difference that made was the rod bent even more alarmingly.

The fish was now 'sounding', heading for the bottom some 300 feet below. "Go on Keith, gi' it sum," Roy encouraged. I was 'gi'ing it plenty! The heat was making my skin leak and I was soaked in perspiration from head to toe. Roy and the two Jacks were sitting back drinking Gatorade. "You carry on, we're having our lunch. You're doing a great job. We reckon it's a oooge sail," said Roy.

Twenty minutes later, with a still-unseen fish now towing the boat – even on just 20 pound line it happens – I was becoming thirstier and hungrier.

"Let's 'av a go," said Roy, taking the rod. A minute later he called Jack S to take over. "Waddya reckon Jack?" he said. "Well, it's a sail for sure," was the response and I, who had never even seen a sailfish, took the rod back. "Let Captain Jack have a go," came the order, so I did and picked up my Gatorade and sandwich from the cooler. Twenty seconds later the rod was jammed into the rod holder, fending for itself. "That's no sailfish," said the experienced captain. By now Roy and Jack S were giggling like 12-year-old girls at a McFly gig. "What is it then captain?" I whispered, sandwich in mid-bite. "Goddam big shark. You'll never see it for sure though," came the reply.

As well as a sailfish, I had never caught a 'goddam big shark' either and being told I would lose it for sure, after what had already been an epic 60-minute war, encouraged me to prove him wrong. I struggled to lever the rod free from the holder – the reel drag was drum-tight and the rod was bent at an angle that rods shouldn't really be bent to – and started again.

Half an hour later I told the three, sitting quietly under the t-top in the shade, that I was winning. I might as well have told them the world's funniest joke judging by the response but when about a hundred yards behind the boat, that evocative shape of a shark's fin appeared, with my line pointing directly at it, they became somewhat more interested. The hook was attached by 80 pound breaking strain mono, with 20 pound mainline. No wire was in the trace and sharks have got some teeth, as we know.

"It'll bite you off in a minute, just cut the line," spake the captain.

"Jack, this fish is coming in," I countered, just as the tail appeared,

The best excuse for loafing in the countryside

thrashed the surface and dived downwards. I had screwed the drag even tighter and held the rod almost pointing at the fish to exert FULL power – and it responded, surfacing maybe 10 yards away and looking knackered. It was a big hammerhead shark, 10 feet long, which we estimated at 250 pounds and, sure enough, like a dog on a lead, I drew it alongside where Roy clicked away with the camera while Capt Jack held its massive head above water, by holding the line with an armoured glove I hasten to add. The hook was right in the corner of the jaw, clear of the row after row of razor-sharp snaggle-teeth and he reached down with his hook-out, muttering: "There, you son-of-a-bitch; we whipped your ass good." To be honest I didn't think there was that much 'we' to it. I had simply been my dogmatic self and proved my point. The legend of Harry the Hammerhead was born and the story remains part of our rituals undertaken on our annual trip to Paradise.

Keith Arthur

Big Fish, Blue Water

In 1996 Sky Sports screened highlights of the Marlin World Cup competition
for the first time. The event, organised by the Sun Resort hotel chain and
Air Mauritius, takes place on one of the most beautiful places imaginable,
Mauritius in the Indian Ocean. A few weeks before the event one of the *Tight
Lines* team, Rob Wakeling who now produces *Soccer AM* on Sky Sports, asked
me how it felt to be going to a tropical paradise and work with one of my
heroes, Allan Lamb the South African-born England cricketer. I had heard
nothing about it and thought that he'd let the cat slip out of the bag. When
they left without me I could have reinserted the cat somewhere slightly less
salubrious about young Rob's person. All I got was the voice-over job when
the film was edited down from the five days of fishing. The following year I
actually made the trip.

It is a long flight to Mauritius and I turned right when getting on the
plane, unlike the stars, who all made the left turn into Club or First Class and
when we touched down from the overnight journey I was pretty worn out,
especially as the queues at immigration were long, then we had to wait for
our official transport in the blistering sun of a Mauritian high summer, early
December. When we arrived at La Pirogue Hotel I soon relaxed in the air-
conditioned cottage that forms the standard rooms at this magnificent resort.

As resident expert on *Tight Lines* and the man responsible for presenting the links filmed on site, as well as voicing over the finished production, I was elevated, for angling purposes, to 'celebrity' status and allocated to a team to compete in the five days of fishing. My team was from the UK division of Acclaim Games, a computer games company, then riding high. The team consisted of staff who had performed well and been rewarded with places on this most wonderful of events as reward. None of them had ever held a fishing rod before and here they were, about to attempt to catch the biggest, most powerful and potentially dangerous fish in the world: the blue marlin.

These members of the billfish clan can reach weights of over 2000 pounds, almost a ton, although none have been boated of that size, mostly because no angler or tackle is sufficient to fight these giants. There is a story I read in *Marlin* magazine where a crew from Abacos in the Bahamas fought a fish estimated at between 1400 and 1800 pounds for 33 hours and 12 minutes before it broke the 600 pound breaking strain leader. The angler could go on no more and instructed the 'wire man', the crew member whose job it is to grab the leader to control the fish for either gaffing or releasing, to "... stop it or pop it" after having the fish close to the boat but out of gaff range on 60 occasions. The wire man took the leader three turns around a cleat at the stern, the fish lunged and popped the line! I wasn't hoping for that, especially as it might be me in the fighting chair for a long session.

Our first requirement was to acquaint the team with how to use the tackle to fight the fish. Marlin are caught over deep water either on live or dead fish bait, or big lures which are towed behind the boat in a special pattern, known as a spread, with between four and seven lures. The line is released until the lures are sitting on top of, or just ahead of, the crest of waves formed by the boat's wake, which is quite substantial as a trolling speed of 9-12mph is maintained. Two lines are fished from long outriggers stretching from the

Keith Arthur

side of the boat at a 90° angle – some boats run four lures from 'riggers'; one is sometimes fished from a line clipped behind the flying bridge dead centre of the wake, way back often 100 yards or more. The remaining lures are fished as 'flatlines', one on each quarter of the stern and from rods set at an angle to the side of the boat, keeping them all separate. The captain then steers the boat down the swell, with the wind, as much as possible, usually traversing the waves on the run upwind. Billfish will almost invariably swim with the wind/swell so are tempted to follow the lures which bubble and burst through the surface, supposedly imitating a school of flying fish, immature tuna or mahi-mahi.

The lines are set in release clips or elastic bands that break out when a fish intercepts the lure, with the reel's drag set tight enough to make the large hook penetrate the bony jaw or bill of the aggressor. The custom in Mauritius when a fish is hooked is to 'gun' the boat's motor to maximum revs to take any remaining stretch from the line, firmly set the hook and attempt to turn the fish towards the boat. It isn't always successful!

The second method, popular with crews because less fuel and effort is used, is using live or dead bonito, members of the tuna family that grow up to maybe 30 pounds in weight in the Indian Ocean, as bait. Bonito swim in huge shoals and feed on even smaller fish, driving them to the surface and smashing into the shoal. Gulls and gannets are attracted and dive down, eating the small fish from above. The birds give the fishes' presence away and at least one crew member spends most of the day scanning the skies ahead looking for bird activity.

I suggested to the crew that we look for birds in an attempt to catch livebaits, which would at least give my team-mates an opportunity to hold a rod and turn a reel handle. We decided that Annie, the lady member of the team, would have first go should we be successful and as soon as a flock of birds were spotted, Annie was seated in the 'fighting chair', a very important piece of equipment on a big-game boat. The chair has a slippery seat, usually fibreglass, although before that became popular some magnificent hardwood chair seats were in use and the very top-of-the-range boats still use chairs with solid teak seats and backrests. In front of the seat, set between the angler's legs is a cup for the rod butt, set on a pin that will allow the cup to rock back and forth. Inside the cup is a gimbal that matches a groove on the rod butt, so the rod cannot rotate. As we approached the bonito shoal the crew wound in the flatlines – leaving out the riggers and shotgun lure at the back, replacing them with lighter rods and small feather lures with weighted heads that were trolled through the melee of feeding bonito. One rod was left to fish whilst I and two of the boat's crew held the other rods, working the lures to attract a bite. My lure was hit; I set the hook and pushed the rod into the gimbal and Annie's hands.

I helped guide Annie through the fight – even on 50 pound class rods and reels bonito pull like crazy – but after 10 minutes she appeared to be making little headway, despite puffing and panting, obviously expending a lot of effort. "This must be what giving birth feels like!" she said, while I and her remaining male team members started ribbing her tardiness at boating what was to be our bait. Eventually the fish came alongside and the crew started shaking their heads. It was quite simply the most massive bonito I had ever seen, and I've not seen another like it since. Not only had it taken ages, but at close to 30 pounds was too big – by about 20 pounds!

We went back to the lures and Neil, the team-captain instructed me that should we get a strike, I was to fight the fish. Having never caught a marlin, this was the stuff of dreams. The boats all have comfortable cabins and the rest of the team sat inside, out of the fierce sun, eating the fruit from packed lunches and keeping liquid levels up: I stood watching the lures, making insignificant adjustments to the position of the flat lines.

We had passed the massive Le Morne headland, where two currents meet, forcing small fish up from the depths which, in turn, attracts predators, and were heading up the east coast. One of the crew was explaining in pidgin English that the buildings on the shore, maybe three miles away, formed a tea plantation when a 'crack' occurred as the line snapped out of the starboard rigger. The captain automatically gunned the boat but there was no fish. I told him that I had been watching much of the time and seen nothing but felt that we should make the run again. The line was reset and five minutes later he made a slow turn and went back over the same ground. The same thing happened again only this time I was REALLY studying the lures. It was the same rig, so we felt that, maybe, the clip retaining the line needed tightening. Just to be on the safe side, we made another 180° turn and at what must have been VERY close to the original spot I saw an explosion on the starboard rigger lure, with white water thrown up all around, and the line snapped out of the tight clip, with the reel singing as the fish made off.

The crewman next to me was screaming what sounded like: "Bully, bully bully" and a massive gulp of black smoke burst from the boat's exhaust as the diesel engine was given full power. The rest of the team were out of the cabin, I was holding the rod, jerking the hook in, much to the disgust of the crew who would rather trust the boat's burst of speed. Two hundred yards away, in the wash of the boat, a blue marlin was dancing across the waves.

Experienced big-game fishermen have names for the specific leaps that marlin make: this one tailwalked, where the fish appears to stand on its tail and swim; it greyhounded, making low leaps and head-and-tailing, similar to the running action of a greyhound. It leapt straight up, it stuck its head out, bill flashing in the sun with the pink lure thrown from the hook way up the line. The hook was in the bill and wasn't coming out! I was in the chair making an attempt to control all this and I can honestly say that I have never, ever been so excited. I felt that at any time my heart would leap from behind my ribcage. The power of a blue marlin has to be experienced before any idea of the force they exert can be imagined.

Twenty-five minutes later the most beautiful sight any angler can envisage was lying beside the boat. The fish change colour during the fight, a phenomenon generated by special cells on the fishes' skin: beside the boat the colour had changed from the silver and blue stripes of aggression to a wonderful lavender shade, merging into a pewter belly, via a copper flank. The eye was as blue as a cornflower in a summer meadow.

The rules of the contest allowed for fish under 200 pounds to be released but count as 200 pounds on the scoresheet. I estimated the fish at less than 200 pounds, even though I'd never seen one alive. I'd seen sharks and tarpon that were either bigger or came close. The captain insisted it was closer to 250 pounds and wanted to gaff the fish, killing it for the weigh-in. If it had been just my fish, the hooks would have been cut and the fish allowed to swim away but I had the team to think of, as well as the crew who earned a bonus for bringing in a fish that is 100% used, with no waste at all, either as food from the flesh, leather (from the skin), oil from the liver and ornaments from the pectoral fins, bill, tail and even the eyes which are turned into souvenir paperweights! The gaff went in, the fish was killed – a far more dignified death than gasping life away in a cold fish box – and lay in the bottom of the boat. At the dock the scales confirmed my estimate: 183 pounds. Not only had we killed the fish unnecessarily, it had cost us the equivalent of 17 pounds-worth of points! I paid the local taxidermist, Mr Bhoogeloo (honestly!) to mount the bill for me and it sits in my office to this day, a brass plaque commemorating the experience.

That wasn't the end of the day either: we went on to bag a big hammerhead shark of 317 pounds that took a live bonito, so we weighed in two fish for exactly 500 pounds!

I have only caught two more marlin since that first, fabulous fish; both have been bigger too but the experience of that fish will live with me until I draw my final breath. It is easy to see how Ernest Hemingway compared fishing for marlin to bullfighting because by no means is the angler guaranteed to win. Marlin kill anglers and, especially, wiremen, every year and deserve their place at the very pinnacle of an angler's potential achievements.

After the Marlin World Cup fell out of television favour, it was replaced by the Shark Cup; a tournament based around a team from Britain (including the Isle of Man), the Brits, taking on the Americans, the Yanks, in their own backyard of Long Island, New York. Montauk, the town on the eastern end of Long Island, is the spiritual home of shark fishing in the USA, thanks mostly to the exploits and marketing of one Frank Mundus. Although Peter Benchley has always denied it, there can be little doubt that Capt Mundus was the inspiration behind Capt Quint in the book and film *Jaws*. In 1986 Frank Mundus brought in a great white shark well in excess of the world record, 3427 pounds, caught on legal tackle but with illegal bait. Before that he had made shark fishing popular across the USA, starting with his local port of Montauk, by describing it as 'Fishing for Monsters', without naming the species. Back in the day, Americans didn't practice much catch and release and as sharks weren't particularly edible – especially when there were tuna, grouper, striped bass and other great eating fish about – they didn't think much of paying large sums to fish for simply trophies. Mundus changed that.

The first two years of the Shark Cup saw the Brits triumph, despite the Yanks having not only home advantage but some of the most successful sea anglers in history on their side. One of those was Herb 'The Rat' Rattner who, at the time I fished with him, had held 161 world records. The Americans do have rather a lot of world records in fishing, more even than boxing, including line classes for many species and tippet strength for fly fishing for those species. Herb played the cards well and knew what records were vulnerable. One of his, for example, is the tiger shark, an extremely aggressive member of the shark clan. Herb holds two line class records, the most impressive being a fish of 255 pounds+ on 6 pound breaking strain line. A tiger shark that heavy will be maybe 9 feet long, the tackle being more suited to catching tench on an English estate lake!

Our day together was on board *My Mate* captained by former NYPD cop Joe McBride, who sat on the fly bridge with a thick cigar in his lips whilst instructing Peter, *his* mate, in what to do next. It was easy to see why Herb caught so many big fish: he was predatory with the tackle, ensuring he had 'best shot' as often as possible. In fact he whupped my ass, as they have this habit of saying across the pond. I did have the last laugh though.

With 15 minutes to go, Herb hooked a big blue shark – Montauk holds the world All-Tackle record for those too: 528 pounds caught on *Half Back*, another boat in the event, captained by Al Cortez. In home waters a blue of 150 pounds is exceptional and a rare catch indeed: in Montauk they are less so and the fish Herb was fighting was easily 200 pounds. In my frustration, I was hoping for a bite but my two rods – we fish with two each spaced from the drifting boat at 60 yards, 40 yards, 20 yards and a 'pitch bait', kept in the boat to cast to visible fish – the furthest and second closest had produced lean pickings all day, although we alternated them half-hourly. The far rod Capt Joe fished with a big livebait, a striped bass of maybe 9 pounds, with two party balloons semi-inflated holding the bait at 40 feet deep. With five minutes of the day left, I was scanning the ocean looking for signs and had even reeled in the second rod, in case another fish did what Herb's had done and attacked the 'chum bucket', a perforated drum of minced fish that lets out a slick attracting the fish. It was then I saw a fin – at least I thought it was a fin.

The day before we had been entertained by an ocean sunfish, mola mola, which had stayed with us for 45 minutes, off the stern, feeding on jellyfish drifting in our wind lane. When I first saw it approaching, I thought it was a shark as the dorsal (top) fin appeared above the waves. I thought we had a reoccurrence and said to Peter, the mate: "Look, a sunfish out by the livebait rod." Capt Joe heard and from his lofty perch shouted: "That's a thrasher, a THRASHER! GRAB THE ROD!!!!"

I needed no second bidding, what I had seen, rather than the dorsal fin of a mola mola, was the tip of the thresher shark's tail. It rose higher from the water then started threshing, or thrashing depending on accent, the water, the bass having swum to the surface to escape. The bass could be seen attempting to swim away but the shark was on its case – and just three minutes of the day remained, plus 45 minutes 'fighting time'. Herb's blue shark was released and the balloons holding the bass started to power away from the boat. The reel was out of gear with the ratchet engaged, the clicking, slow at first, soon accelerated to a scream.

"SET THE HOOK, SET THE HOOK!" yelled Joe, so I did, putting the reel into gear and slamming the rod back four or five times to set the hook. The rod I was using is designed for big fish; marlin, big tuna and big sharks and this was one big shark. Suddenly there was an explosion 150 yards from the boat as the massive fish, 8 feet long with a tail about the same size, leapt clear of the water. My heart was pounding fit to burst and with just 45 minutes to fight the fish into submission, I was steeling myself for battle. Around my waist I had a special belt to hold the butt of the rod, similar in design to the cup on a fighting chair and, above that, a harness that clips on to the reel, allowing the body, rather than just the arms, to do some work.

The fish sounded deep almost directly under the boat – we were drifting in 220 feet of water, 25 miles from land. Peter, Joe and, to his eternal credit, Herb were willing me to win and I was pumping the fish for all I was worth, the drag set as hard as I dare, probably at 30 pounds pressure against the 50 pound line. After 15 minutes or so the fish was 25 feet down, 50 feet behind the boat but kept making slow, dogged runs. Then 20 minutes into what had turned from battle to war, the tip of my leader appeared: the fish was 30 feet away. Once the mate touches the leader, the fish is 'caught' but I had a cameraman who wanted to see a thresher shark up close, for the programme's sake.

Once I had the first part of the special 'wind-on' leader in the rod, Peter was able to grab the main section in his gloved hands and steer the fish alongside. It lay there, directly next to the starboard quarter, lazily pulsing its huge, sickle-shaped tail: beautiful dark blue-grey back, merging into copper-coloured flanks and white belly. The cameraman got close-up, focusing right into the small eye that seemed to fix him in a stare directly from Hell. Peter took his unhooking tool and removed the hook from the side of the tooth-filled mouth and watched it slowly slide back to the depths.

I was shot: tears filled my eyes as it is a genuinely emotional experience, for me at least, when such a prehistoric creature is forced to submit, albeit temporarily. Joe estimated the fish at between 350 and 375 pounds, one of only three thresher sharks caught on the tournament. It won me nothing but respect, Herb still outscored me on the day, but it was a genuine fish-of-a-lifetime and one that I doubt I will equal.

To add a large dollop of icing on the cake, I interviewed Frank Mundus the next day, the man being at least as mighty as the legend. Capt Frank Mundus passed away on September 10th 2008 in Hawaii. His memory will live on forever in every angler that casts a line for sharks.

Keith Arthur

Under African Skies

My first journey to Africa came via an invitation to Pemba Channel Fishing Lodge situated on the extreme southern end of Kenya's coastline, almost in Tanzania. The area is famous for its black marlin and sailfish as well as yellowfin tuna, 'ahi' to sushi fans, several shark species including mako and tiger sharks and giant trevally, the ocean's ultimate bully-boy.

The journey was best described as interesting, the Kenya Airways 747 –travelling by 'jumbo' means something else I guess –taking us as far as Nairobi then an internal flight would carry us on to Mombasa, the final part of the journey from there would be by road. As this was to be filmed for *Tight Lines* I was accompanied by Julia Hunter, the series producer, and John 'Tess' Terrosorio, our Australian cameraman. Our arrival in Nairobi was on time but Jomo Kenyatta Airport came as a bit of a shock. Rundown would be an understatement. Many of the fluorescent lights had gone missing, presumed stolen and there were empty supports and bare wires hanging where once hung television monitors announcing departures and arrivals. I hope they showed something slightly more interesting in the sitting room of the people that stole them!

Some refreshment was in order and a trip to the airport cafe/bar for two 'Tusker' beers, in 500cl bottles and a large espresso (for me!) came to 80 Kenya shillings, or the equivalent of £1. The same things in a Paris airport

Keith Arthur

came to £9, only it was 'biere blonde' and smaller glasses! The remainder
of the journey was slightly more interesting as we boarded our flight to
Mombasa, having watched our bags being loaded first, and were then
'bumped off' it because some Kenyan dignitaries or businessmen turned up
and wanted our seats. That entailed a three-hour wait but the authorities at
least gave us a voucher for a buffet meal in the airport hotel. Beer was more
expensive there!

On arrival at Mombasa we had to find our bags and equipment, which
took some time and a deep reluctance on the part of the customs police to
hand it over. We later learned that a swift bribe sorts out most things when
our driver appeared for the last part of the journey to Shimoni, the village
next to our destination resort. His vehicle came as a bit of a shock: it was a
Mercedes saloon and we had a serious amount of kit, even without my fishing
gear: the lodge supply everything on the boats. Tess's equipment, including a
tripod, several spare camera batteries and chargers, lights and the like take up
a lot of room and the car was rammed out.

Mombasa, which translates to 'City of War' apparently, stands on an island
so we had to take a car ferry across an estuary to leave it. This was interesting
as the 'boat' was more of a large raft, with no sides, not even rails, and cars
and trucks piled on until it was full, foot passengers taking their chances
hanging on to whatever they could. Our driver informed us that 17 people
had recently died when their minibus rolled off into the water, which is
infested with sharks, mostly bull, or Zambezi, sharks that can tolerate fresh
water. The truck in front of us couldn't make the climb up the steep ramp on
the opposite side so it was all hands on deck to push it off.

The next part of the drive came as a complete culture shock, the streets
lined by, literally, mud huts with people selling everything from fried fish, in

The best excuse for loafing in the countryside

the most part carried around in what looked like dustbin lids balanced on Kenyan women's heads, to pots and pans, to trinkets and touristy items. The road was filled with traffic which all seemed to be Toyota minibuses; every seat taken, with other passengers hanging on the roof, wing mirrors or any other appendage. But soon we were free of the city driving along a metalled road between bush. The only wildlife to be seen was baboons and we passed several troops scavenging beside the road.

Then we turned off the road on to a track that just disappeared into the jungle. It was similar to your average farm track: rutted, bumpy, with sharp, blind bends. Occasionally a very ancient pickup truck or jeep would pass in the opposite direction but most of the traffic was either bicycles or people on foot. Suddenly our driver, who spoke no English that we could understand, stopped and ushered us out of the car pointing to the rear nearside wheel, the tyre on which was flatter than your average pancake. He opened the boot and we removed the mountain of gear in it, although some was between Tess and Julia on the back seat, even on their laps – seniority had decreed I took the front seat with just my hand luggage on my knees. Once the boot was emptied he removed the jack and wheel brace, incongruously erected a safety triangle 20 yards back and took off the wheel. He then removed the spare from its trap beneath the boot carpet and found the tyre to be both treadless and as airless as that on the original wheel. Miles from anywhere, in a hot jungle, in clothes we'd worn for over 20 hours, designed for English springtime rather than equatorial Africa, we were stuck with three wheels on our wagon.

Our driver wandered off into the dense bush, returning shortly afterwards with a bloke on a butcher-boy's bike, with a basket on the front. The original wheel was loaded into the basket and off he went, although whether a 'Tyres

Keith Arthur

R Us' existed within 500 miles is debatable. We continued to wait, without a drink, shelter from the sun or much hope of moving. Then one of those miracles that sometimes happen, happened: a jeep, pretty much fully laden, stopped. The white driver spoke to our African driver before getting down from the cab and inviting us to hop in for a lift. He ran the neighbouring fishing lodge to Pemba Channel and had been to Mombasa for the month's shop and we could just about squeeze in between the provisions – but without ANY of our luggage, even a change of clothes – at least we were moving again. Arriving at the wonderful Pemba Channel Fishing Club we showered, were given a new t-shirt to replace our own sweaty garments and plenty of superb fresh fruit juice. Our gear was waiting for us the next morning and we made a couple of great films in just about the most beautiful surroundings imaginable. It was a slight shock on the second morning to see a troop of monkeys in the pool and each night we were woken by bush-babies whistling to each other from our thatched roofs, with hornbills sitting in the branches watching us eat breakfast.

Having been successful and catching a couple of big Indian Ocean sailfish, wahoo and barracuda, on the first two days, our final day's filming was to be along the reef known locally as Kissenganwi to fish for koli-koli and karembesi. Both are members of the trevally clan, the latter being the giant trevally, possibly the fiercest of all fish.

Having trolled lures for an hour with little success apart from two small koli-koli, maybe 12 pounds each, one of the crew spotted some birds 'working' on a school of bait. The small fish were being chased by rainbow runners, a member of the jack family, rated very highly as GT bait when between 12 and 18 inches long. I caught two on lures cast into the melee and the bait-man carefully prepared them for the hook, first gutting, then threading the hook through from mouth to vent before stitching the whole thing up again. These were fished about 30 feet down, by means of a downrigger, a heavy weight, the 'downrigger ball', on the end of very heavy braided line on a powerful reel and tiny, stiff rod. The leader is clipped to the weight, which is lowered to the desired depth, the reel used for fishing releasing line at the same time. The fishing rod is bent into the weight of the downrigger ball so a take can pull the line from the clip, releasing the tension on the rod, indicating a bite.

It didn't take long for that to happen and it took even less time for the reel's drag to scream blue murder as something very nasty swam very quickly away. I was instructed to take the rod from the holder and start pulling! With the reel now quietened and the fish more relaxed into the battle, I had the rod in my buttpad and was taking the strain.

"Would you like a shoulder harness?" asked the captain. I replied that I was fine and that we would soon be seeing whatever was on the hook lying alongside the boat, apologising for eating the bait. Twenty minutes later the situation was unchanged except that sweat was pouring from me, my arms were aching like mad and my back was rapidly catching them up! The bait-man peered over the side and yelled: "Karembesi mister, big karembesi." I looked for myself and there, maybe 40 feet below, swam not one but four BIG fish, one of which was giving me all the trouble I needed, and then some. The most obvious things were the long, pointed pectoral fins protruding from beneath the fishes' gills: these are like stabilisers and were preventing my best efforts from making any impact on the fish at all. Tess was giving me all sorts of grief, saying that these fish were pussycats compared to the squid that his father caught out from Sydney. "That's proper fishing mate," he insisted. "Not cissy-stuff like this."

Keith Arthur

"Maybe I should try the shoulder harness," I whimpered, and the device was fitted. Now, with the harness clipped to the reel, I could use my battered and abused body to increase leverage and after a battle lasting close to an hour, I saw my first giant trevally, sitting on the deck. The fish was killed to be eaten later – Pemba Channel is a LONG way from supermarkets and fish provides most of the diet for the guests. Superbly cooked it is too; I can recommend the wahoo soufflé highly.

That was our filming done so our captain asked if Julia and Tess would like a turn on our final half day, we didn't have to leave until early evening. We were taken out in Falusi, a Bertram Sportfisher, complete with swimming platform and fighting chair and stopped to catch bait soon after leaving the dock. Julia, Tess and I all dived in for a swim, only to be told that the all-Africa tiger shark record had been caught very close to the spot where we were currently splashing about. We got out of the water almost as rapidly as we'd got in it.

With bait on board, we started to troll and Julia had first blood with a bonito, so next bite was Tess's turn, with me acting as crew. Soon the reel was screaming, a fish was on, and Tess picked up the rod, engaging the drag. He was nearly pulled over the side as whatever had taken the bait wasn't enjoying eating it much.

"Jeez mate, it's a monster!" Tess proclaimed. "Better get me that harness thing." Five minutes later he was in the fighting chair, puffing like an old steam engine, begging me to take the rod. "Don't worry mate, it's only cissy fishing," I replied. Eventually a yellowfin tuna appeared beside the boat – more dinner table fare – all of 15 pounds in weight. "Great pal, you've caught the bait, let's see if there's a marlin out here," I suggested.

"Bait? You're joking! That's gotta be 50 pounds mate. It's nearly killed me," Tess whined.

Keith Arthur

In all our fishing experiences together following that day, I never heard the word 'cissy' or about the fighting qualities of Sydney squid.

Fishing for sharks from the shore in Namibia is a different thing altogether and when I made my first journey to the Skeleton Coast I could say I wasn't fully prepared for what lay ahead. It is difficult to understand the geography but very easy to explain. Starting at the water's edge is the beach. That continues to the road, anywhere from a hundred yards to a couple of miles away then it is desert: sand is not in short supply.

The target species are bronze whaler sharks, or copper sharks as they are known by the South Africans, who make up most of the anglers, and guides, along the coast. They are there in such numbers and so close in because of a cold current that runs up the coastline from the south bringing with it a super-abundance of sardines. These in turn attract highly sporting edible species such as kob and steenbrass and other shark species, especially small sharks in the form of spotted gully and smoothhound, similar to our own bull huss and common smoothhound. The bronzies prey more on small sharks than other fish and the prime bait is a shark liver although many guides are in full conservation mode and use mackerel baits. A reef runs along the coast, just offshore, resulting in the many skeletons (of ships) that give the region its name and it is through gaps in the reef that the apex predators come hunting. The guides identify the gaps by looking at wave patterns: an area of lower waves indicates deeper water, therefore a gap. As the wind is predominantly onshore due to hot air rising from the sand and cool air rushing in from the ocean to replace it, finding a break is not too difficult: finding a bronzie is rather less easy.

Unbelievably the tackle used is very similar to our standard beach casting gear, with a 13 or 14 foot rod, capable of casting up to 1 pound of weight and bait combined, linked with a multiplier reel loaded with 30 pound monofilament. The business end is a touch more robust with a length of 150 pound mono as a rubbing leader terminating in wire trace with two large single hooks, size 10/0 at least, to hold the bait and hook the shark.

I was in a party with some anglers from the Isle of Man and a Danish angler. During the week we had all caught bronzies, at least one each, and on the last day the Garden Hotel in Walvis Bay, where we were staying, had arranged a special barbecue with local delicacies such as kudu on the menu. As we had all caught sharks and the last day was particularly slow fishing, we quit early to get showered and set for the barbecue and our introduction to The Big Five – more of that shortly. I was with guide Terrance Clark and Kristian from Denmark, driving along the Trans Kalahari Highway towards Swakopmund and then to Walvis Bay. It was around 5pm and as we approached a development of new houses – with a very weird palm tree in the centre which I later learned was a plastic one, holding a mobile telephone aerial – Terrance asked if we'd like the last hour on Langstraand – Long Beach – directly before the new houses. We both agreed and as we parked in the car park a man was swimming in the surf. Rather him than me, I thought: I knew what lived there!

We cast out directly in front of the car park, I was using my own reel, a very expensive Italian job designed for catching marlin and the like on light tackle. It was loaded with 750 yards of brand new 20 pound breaking strain line and I considered that plenty, distance wise anyway. After a few minutes Terrance suggested we reel in as he had two fresh baits ready: we did and recast immediately. Not 10 minutes had passed when I felt my lead lift from the bottom, maybe 70 yards out. This can occasionally be caused by undertow: it's the next 20 seconds that prove vital as if the rod bends, it's game on... the rod bent!

I set the hook by winding down and striking the rod back over my shoulder, running(!) backwards to remove any stretch from the line that could hinder penetration. The bronzie on the other end was not amused and set off for Brazil, a few thousand miles to the west. I had set my drag to 7 pounds, an appreciable amount when multiplied by the leverage of 14 feet of carbon fibre: the shark wasn't interested in that and I watched in dismay as my brand new, bright yellow line simply melted from the spool. I increased the tension on the drag, which made no difference at all; this can be a very risky trick too as the more line that leaves a reel, the greater tension is exerted on it. When the line capacity was just about on the 'fumes' stage, the fish stopped. I estimated something like 80-100 yards remained. Now I had to get some back: the sun was setting and darkness approached. Luckily the fish hadn't gone straight out but had run at an angle so by walking to my right I could retrieve some line and, after a couple of hundred yards struggling through the soft, fine sand, I was in line with the enemy: all I had to do now was bring it in.

Standard practice involves 'pumping'; drawing back the rod and winding the line gained on to the spool. The trouble begins when, with still something like 400 yards of line out there, all this achieves is stretch. Terrance explained that I had to walk backwards, up the beach towards the highway, then run back, winding as I go. I am not particularly athletic, especially when running through soft sand, winding on line to a reel attached to a long, heavy sea rod. It hurt like hell; my calf muscles were wondering what had hit them and my lungs weren't that impressed either. But there was a big fish on the end and I don't give up easily.

By now the sun had set and it was dark. How dark is difficult to explain if you have never been anywhere a very long way from the nearest street lamp or other form of light pollution. Kristian was instructed to start the jeep, turn on the lights and drive so as to keep the yellow line in the headlamps' glow. We were close to two hours into the battle and my stomach was beginning to worry about the kudu being overdone. My brain was starting to worry about my body being done in!

Then what seemed an awfully long way out in the breakers, Terrance saw a tail; my shark's tail. Several feet in front of it was my shark's dorsal fin: this was a very big fish indeed. Where Terrance gets his bravery from I don't know, unless it's from the Foolhardy department store, as he picked up his long-handled gaff (the sharks are gaffed in the dorsal fin, brought to the shore for measuring and then released) and waded into the darkness of the surf, as far as above the waist in the wave's trough, above his head on the crests. He managed to hook the line with the gaff and began, slowly and inexorably pulling the fish closer. It was now clearly visible in the waves and simply refused to turn head-on, although as that would have put Terrance's body and its teeth in collision course, it was no bad thing. I could see the double-line, and the leader, both just out of Terrance's reach. I was still maintaining tension at my end; walking backwards, then limping forwards. Then the line parted: after two hours and 20 minutes the fish was lost. Terrance had done all he could, indeed MORE than he should but to no avail. I often wonder what would have happened if he had managed to put the gaff into the huge fish's fin. The gaff was held by a lanyard around his wrist and if the line had broken and the fish had swum away, he would have gone with it so maybe it was a blessing in disguise.

I felt that we all had done our very best and I had seen the fish, felt its power and it had won: sometimes we have to accept second place.

Luckily the rest of the crowd and the staff at The Garden had saved us some barbecue and we celebrated after eating our fill by meeting The Big Five. These are the species most sought-after on safari: Lion, water buffalo, leopard, elephant and rhinoceros and they are produced in the confines of the Garden bar in the form of cocktails. It can get a bit messy, and it did.

Glossary of Terms

When answering a question on a phone-in programme called *Fisherman's Tales* on the dear-departed *Wire TV*, I was describing the intricacies of waggler fishing when the presenter, Nicky Horne, said:

"Hang on a minute: what's a waggler?"

That was to be the title of this chapter but, having read several posh, scientific-type books, I noticed that they had what is known as a 'Glossary of Terms". So I thought I'd have one, as well. Let's kick off with:

Angling: The art of catching fish using a hook. (Saxon *angul* = hook)...

MISCELLANEOUS:

Draw: 1/ The meeting place designated by the organisers for a competition. 2/ The act of randomly pulling a numbered ball or ticket from a hat or other suitable vessel.

Draw-bag: 1/ One type of container for peg numbers. 2/ Nickname, often fuelled by jealousy of an angler with the innate ability to draw a flyer; as in: "He's a right drawbag."

Weigh-in: Fish caught during a competition are retained in a keepnet. Following the end of the match a designated scalesman weighs each angler's fish in turn and either the angler with the heaviest catch or, if you believe some people, the scalesman's best mate, wins the match.

Flyer: The peg that everyone predicts will win the match. Also, the peg that actually wins the match but no one predicted it beforehand. It becomes a flyer in the café afterwards.

Peg: On a competition anglers randomly pull a numbered ball or ticket from a hat or other suitable vessel. This designates where they shall fish, that place marked on the bank by a 'peg', which can vary from a proper peg stuck in the ground to a piece of paper or raffle ticket, possibly the other half of the draw ticket, placed under a stone. Some pegs of this type have been known to wander with the angler first on the scene often ending up on a flyer.

Float fishing: A style of fishing using a float to suspend a bait at a given depth, even on the bed of a lake or river. The float also indicates a bite, usually by going down. Anglers buy floats because they look good and are individually quite inexpensive. It is impossible to have too many. Floats are said to catch more fish than anglers, a truism which also applies to flies.

FLOATS:

Porcupine quill: One of the sharp things which porcupines have sticking out of them, used as floats before decent stick floats were available. The most common are white at the tip end and dark at the other, the dark being dead quill, therefore denser and sinking. The white top bit is alive and buoyant, so the float is self-cocking. All-white quills, 'albinos', were prized possessions as they carried more split shot. Two friends of mine tried to get some cheap 'porcys' once and went to London Zoo for that purpose. The porcupines weren't that co-operative.

Bottom-end (also 'peg-leg'): A means of attaching floats at the base so the line could be sunk below the surface, out of the way of the wind. Eventually became known as 'fishing the waggler'.

Stick: A float designed by Benny Ashurst and made with a balsa wood top and lignum (*lignum vitae*) cane base, the lignum bases coming from the spindles in the old Lancashire cotton mills. Self-cocking and originally designed for canals, they proved perfect for presenting small baits naturally on fast-flowing rivers, especially the Trent where they were first introduced. Old policemen's truncheons were made from lignum but were too large for stick floats. When Robert Tesse watched Kevin Ashurst fishing 'the stick' on the Trent, he asked journalist Colin Dyson with a chuckle: "Why do they call it a stick? Does he beat the other anglers with it?" To which Dyson replied: "All too bloody often!"

Waggler: The late Trent angler Johnny Rolfe is credited with being the first to fish a bottom-end float on a river. He designed his own and called them 'swingers', because they swung on the line. Kevin Ashurst, son of the late Benny, above, saw Rolfey using one and said in his thick Leigh, Lancs, accent: "Thah don't swing; looks more lahk waggle ter me." And the name was born!

Pilot: In the old days of pike fishing, when using a bung float, a small, egg-shaped float was left to slide on the line above the bung. When the pike made its first run, that the angler let happen allowing the fish to first turn the bait and then swallow – most pike were taken home for tea in those days – the pilot float showed where the fish was going, allowing the angler to strike should it go near snags or gauge how powerful the strike needed to be to set the hooks.

Bung: Also called 'Fishing Gazette Pike Float", this is an egg-sized and shaped piece of cork (traditionally), drilled centrally and slit on one side to allow the bung to be set at a depth, the line passed to the centre via the slit, then stopped in place with a suitable piece of dowel. Usually painted red on the top and varnished, the floats were so big that often bites could be heard as a distinct 'perlop' as the float was pulled under by a feeding pike.

Self-cocking: When the correct amount of weight is applied to a float to make it stand in the water to indicate bites, it is said to be cocked. A self-cocking float has the weight built in to the base. And you thought it was going to be something naughty.

Legering: A style of fishing that uses a weight to take the bait to the bottom and, usually, keep it there. Sometimes a floating bait can be used with the leger weight used as an anchor. This is known as 'zig-rigging' in modern angling parlance.

LEGERS & WEIGHTS:

Split shot: Once lead, since 1987 when most sizes of lead shot became illegal because of dangers to swans – not for the obvious reason, through being shot with them from a gun but because swans forage on gravel close to the bank and ingesting lead shot poisons them – made from other much more expensive and far less functional metals and alloys, these are used to cock the float by inserting the line into a split cut into the side, which is then squeezed closed. The sizes, which sound complicated, from largest to smallest: SSG, AAA, BB, then numbers from 1 to 13, are the sizes of shotgun pellets, which were the original source. Ironically lead shot is still in common use in shotgun cartridges but no one has told the swans.

Coffin: A weight, shaped like a coffin, drilled centrally, longways. Used for holding bottom in the dead centre of a strong-flowing river.

Drilled bullet: Bullet as in musket-ball. Spherical weight, drilled centrally, used for rolling a bait on a river. Has a strong habit of rolling straight into snags and weed.

Bomb: 1/ Generic term for legering without a swimfeeder. 2/ A pear-shaped weight. Richard Walker invented a special bomb named after Arlesey Lake in Bedfordshire that incorporated a swivel built into the thin end of the pear. This weight could be cast long distances and, because of the built-in swivel, eliminate tangles.

Swimfeeder: A weighted, plastic device used to hold bait and release it when it reaches the lake or river bed. Many types are available including 'open end': with open ends used for groundbait; 'blockend': with one end sealed and the other end capped so it can be filled from one end. Most common bait used is maggots which, in theory, wriggle out when on the lake or river bed. Other, inert, baits are used which usually come out either as the blockend hits the water or on the retrieve, especially in still water, although many anglers believe otherwise.

Line: Usually monofilament but sometimes braided material that joins the angler to the fish, via the hook, until it breaks. See 'breaking strain'.

Breaking strain: The amount of force required to break the line. This is usually slightly less than the biggest fish of the day/year/angling career can muster, resulting in 'the one that got away'.

Knot: Once described as: "A tangle with a name." There are hundreds of angling knots most of which are wrong at one time or another. One commonly used knot is called a no-knot because, technically, it isn't a knot at all.

Hooks: A piece of metal bent into a shape designed to stay fixed in a fish's mouth. Some of the names of the shapes include: Round bend, crystal bend, Limerick, O'Shaughnessy. I have no idea why.

Size: The smallest hooks have the highest number: a size 20 is roughly a 1/10 scale model of a size 1. The sizes then go UP in number with a 0 behind, so a 4/0 is considerably larger than a size 1 and MUCH bigger than a size 4. This can confuse. Unsurprisingly.

Treble hook: This has three tines and is commonly used when fishing for predatory species to ensure a hook-up. Traditionally fixed to lures and used when live or dead fish are the bait, with one tine in the bait so, hopefully, the other two can somehow snag the target fish.

Spade-end: A hook on which the wire is flattened at the opposite end to the point so the line can be whipped to the shank to attach it.

Eyed: A hook with an eye, or hole, where the other one has a spade-end. Line is passed through the eye and knotted, sometimes with a no-knot.

Barbless: Many hooks are made with a barb set slightly below the point of the hook. Others have no barb and are called barbless. They are easy to remove, especially by the fish themselves(!) and the majority of heavily-stocked fisheries insist on their use. It seems that the more fish a fishery contains, the harder the rules make catching them.

Shank: The part of the hook from the spade or eye to the bend.

FISH SPECIES NICKNAMES:

Skimmers: Small bream, usually less than 1 pound in weight on canals, 2 pound in weight elsewhere. On canals a bream between the weight of 1 and 2 pounds would generally be described as a big skimmer. A 'skimmer' over 3 pounds is a bream anywhere!

TACKLE:

Landing net: A net, usually round or triangular, attached to a pole (landing net handle) and used to lift hooked fish from the water.

Keepnet: A long, either circular or rectangular net used to retain fish once caught. Minimum legal length is 2 metres. Anyone who says they've caught a 'net-full' is exaggerating although it is common parlance amongst anglers and could be a reason why they are often thought to exaggerate.

Rod rest: A device to rest the rod on whilst awaiting a bite. Some species are known for the violence of the bite and on many occasions have dragged rods from their rests, never to be seen again.

Spinners/lures: Metal, wood or plastic, these are artificial baits intended to fool fish into eating them. Like floats they are more likely to attract the angler into buying them.

Flies: Similar to lures but made of soft materials such as fur, feather and tinsel. Addictive.

Bait dropper: A small cage with a trap door used to lower baits to the river or lake bed. The end without a door is attached to the hook and the trap door opens when reaching the bottom by means of a lever beneath the door. Sounds more complicated than it is.

Swivel: A metal device, varying in size from 5 centimetres to 30 centimetres. The line is attached to either end via an eye (see eyed hooks) and each end can rotate independently, preventing line twist. Sounds more complicated than it is.

Snap swivel: As above with a safety-pin type clip at one end so a lure, leger weight, float or other device can be attached.

Rods: High-tech pieces of angling equipment, suitably priced, that enable us to catch fish. As with floats and flies it is impossible to have too many.

Float rod: A rod designed for fishing with a float on the line. Usually between 4 metres and 6 metres long.

Leger rod: A rod designed for legering: usually between 3 and 4 metres long. Stronger than most float rods.

Carp rod: Designed to catch carp: usually between 3.5 and 4 metres long and at least three are used at a time by 'real' carp anglers.

Roach pole: A rod used without a reel with the line attached to the thin end, most commonly to a length of special elastic housed within the top 2 metres of the pole. Poles are often in excess of 15 metres long but are most commonly used at 10 to 11 metres. Can cost up to £3000 and are not (fortunately) as addictive as other tackle items but need replacing when a newer model comes out. Often this will be very similar except in graphics on the butt section.

Rings including butt ring: Guides fixed to the rod for the line to run through. Once all-metal, now mostly metal rings containing very expensive, high-tec ceramic linings made from (allegedly) materials such as 'silicon carbide', 'titanium oxide' and 'aluminium oxide'. Whether these materials exist in reality is irrelevant: they make great rod rings. The 'butt ring', you will be relieved to know, is nothing more sinister than the name of the guide closest to the reel.

Reels: The machine used for holding line, fixed close to the fat end of the rod. They come in the following styles:

Centrepin: The 'traditional' reel with the spool containing the line revolving around a central spindle. The spool revolves to let line peel off and is wound back on by rotating the spool in the opposite direction.

Fixed spool: The most common form of reel in use today. The spool faces the front and line is wound on via a bail arm like the spinning jenny. The spool stays still. The bail arm is lifted to allow the line to fall from the spool. Line is wound back by turning a handle that rotates the bail arm on a rotor system. Sounds more complicated than it is.

Multiplier: A reel with a rotating spool and a gear system so one turn of the handle can rotate the spool several times. Has the benefits of holding large amounts of line so big multipliers are used for the biggest fish, such as sharks, marlin etc. Sounds less complicated than it is.

Bail arm: A stiff wire bent to a shape so line nestles in one corner, often with a roller. Attached to a rotor behind the spool. The reel handle is turned to rotate the rotor and the bail arm guides the line on to the spool. Sounds more complicated than it is.

Slipping clutch/drag: A mechanism built into the reel, both fixed spool and multiplier that yields line under a pre-set tension. Poor quality drags or those badly set result in lost fish, so another great excuse!

Baits: Items both natural and artificial with which anglers hope to catch fish. The very best excuse for a bad day is: 'the wrong bait'.

Maggots: Fly larvae used alive in normal circumstances. 'Normal' maggots are bluebottle larvae, 'pinkies' are greenbottle larvae, which have a pinkish tinge whilst 'squatts' are housefly larvae. All are bred commercially on maggot farms that possibly reduce the value of adjoining property because they pong! Sold into tackle shops in gallon measures that, in all other forms, are eight pints. Maggots tend to be in seven pints because, as any bait dealer will tell you: "They shrink." Tackle shops sell them in pint measures. Maggots can be dyed various colours, the most popular currently is red. The dye is added to the food in the growing process. Once maggots are full-grown they leave the food and are ready for 'harvest'. Except squatts, which are vegetarian and can be encouraged to 'eat' dampened bread. Maggots sink in water when dry but float when a tiny amount of water is added before throwing them in. But they NEVER float to the surface after being submerged when fishing. Whether this is because fish eat them all (unlikely) or it is just one of life's great mysteries is unclear. Squatts FLOAT when dry and sink when wet. This sounds complicated and it is.

Casters: The pupa formed when maggots transform into flies. Used as bait in the early stages of transformation the bluebottle variety sink. Developed as a bait by Benny Ashurst (see 'floats' above).

Lobworms: Large earthworms. These are best gathered on muggy, dark nights when they come to the surface of grassy areas to meet another worm for procreation. Worms are hermaphrodite but need to be fertilised by another. They conjoin through a muscley band around their body, commonly known as 'the saddle'.

Brandlings: Smaller than lobworms, brandlings live and breed in manure heaps. Identifiable by a yellow banding around the body of the otherwise dull red-coloured worm.

Dendrabenas: Commercially-bred worms, vegetarian in nature, with similar bands but paler yellow, almost white in colour, to brandlings.

Bloodworm: Aquatic larvae of the gnat, found in the silt on the bed of slightly polluted lakes.

Joker: Aquatic larvae of the midge, found in the silt of sewage outfalls. Most bloodworm and joker is imported from mainland Europe as we have cleaned up our sewage works. Both bloodworm and joker are banned on many waters. The often-held belief of many anglers is that the bans are imposed by those who can't be bothered to learn how to use the baits.

Hemp: Hemp seed produces cannabis plants but not, apparently, that used by anglers – the hemp that is. A grain of hemp is usually between 3.5 and 5 millimetres in diameter: the largest hemp comes traditionally from Chile, the smallest from China. Banned on many waters for several reasons: "It dopes the fish." (Unlikely as it is boiled.) "It grows on the bottom." (Unlikely as it is boiled.) "Once a fish has eaten it nothing else will catch them." (Unlikely because it isn't a natural diet.) Hemp is a common bird food and birds that eat it show no signs of addiction. Nor do birds that smoke it!

Tares: A very hard seed used primarily as birdfood, 5 or 6 millimetres in diameter that, like hemp, has to be boiled to make them soft enough to hook. Most commonly used in conjunction with hemp as feed. Ironically not banned anywhere that I am aware of.

Groundbait: *(verb)*. To groundbait means to throw in bait to attract fish to eat what is on the hook. Usually this refers to groundbait *(noun)*: Commonly cereal crumbs (bread, biscuit, cake), dampened so it will sink, formed into balls and thrown, catapulted or carried in a swimfeeder to the precise spot where the baited hook is placed. More myth and legend surrounds groundbait, with reference to exotic ingredients ('champagne biscuits') and additives ('synthetic pheromones') for example. One famous angler, the late Ivan Marks was often accused of using additives that were secret so with his business partner Roy Marlow, Marks produced a groundbait called Secret Squirrel that sold by the tonne! Some anglers insisted it contained squirrel droppings whereas it was, in fact, more in the line of the bovine variety.

... and end with:

The best excuse for loafing in the countryside

Keith Arthur

Fishing: The best excuse for loafing in the countryside.

Keith Arthur 2009